THE **REAL** HEALTH RECIPE BOOK

Other books by David A. Phillips

From Soil to Psyche, USA, 1975
The Soil to Psyche Recipe Book, USA, 1975
Guide Book to Nutritional Factors in Edible Foods, Sydney, 1977
Guidebook to Nutritional Factors in Foods, USA, 1979
Secrets of the Inner Self, Sydney, 1980
New Dimensions in Health, Sydney, 1983
Recipes for Health and Pleasure, USA, 1983

THE **REAL** HEALTH RECIPE BOOK

A Vegetarian Guide to Health Foods

Dr David A. Phillips

DOUBLEDAY
Sydney & Auckland

The Real Health Recipe Book

Published in Australasia in 1986 by
Doubleday Australia Pty Limited
91 Mars Road, Lane Cove, NSW 2066

Offset by arrangement and kind permission of
Angus & Robertson Publishers

Previously published by Angus & Robertson
under the title of
The New Dimensions Recipe Book

National Library of Australia
Cataloguing in Publication data

Phillips, David A., 1934–
Real health recipe book.

Includes index,
ISBN 0 86824 277 2

1. Vegetarian cookery. 2. Food, Natural. I. Phillips, David A., 1934– . New dimensions recipe book. II. Title. III. Title: New dimensions recipe book.

641.5'636

Printed and bound in Hong Kong by
Mandarin Offset Marketing (H.K.) Ltd.

Contents

My Wish

May every reader share in the enjoyment with which the contents of this book have provided me and my family and friends.

Every recipe has been tested in my own kitchen, tasted and enjoyed by many of my friends (who have not deserted me since), and unanimously approved by everyone involved in the testing and preparation.

I do hope all readers of this book enjoy its products as much as we, who were involved in its production, did. Happy, healthy eating.

David A. Phillips
North Sydney, NSW

Preface

Previous incarnations of this book

When initially completed in 1976 as *The Soil to Psyche Recipe Book,* my unique recipe book concept drew scores of favourable reviews from health writers in the USA, where it was published by Woodbridge Press Publishing Company. It also drew a critical review from a non-vegetarian, salt-and-pepper man who said "it is too strict, too different". That is one of its special virtues.

But the seedbed of creative recipes continued to flourish after the initial publication and new and modified recipes began to accumulate in my scrap-book after repeated refinements in the kitchen and constructive suggestions from the dining room. So the need for a further recipe book was born. Its timing was to closely follow the release of my greatly-expounded health manual entitled *New Dimensions in Health,* published by Angus and Robertson Publishers in Sydney in 1983.

Therefore, it seemed only natural to call the second incarnation of the recipe book, *The New Dimensions Recipe Book* which was released in July 1983. But the title did not convey the full story, for this unique recipe book was so much more than 'another beautiful health food recipe book'. Of all such books (and there are many) produced for international readership over the past decade, this is the *only real* health food recipe book.

Further development and refinement brought the book to its present and third incarnation as *The Real Health Recipe Book.* Time now for these recipes to receive the world-wide taste approval that will contribute to the growing realisation that a vegetarian way-of-life offers more variety of flavour and texture, finer fragrances and far greater healthfulness than is ever possible from orthodox Western dietary habits.

Introduction

The Real Health Recipe Book

Why this book is unique

The Real Health Recipe Book is not meant to be a challenge to other health food recipe books or cook books, but by default it will be a challenge to their authors. This book will not be joining the wagon-train of those health consciousness books that invariably fall by the wayside due to inadequate research, insufficient health awareness of the authors or a total misunderstanding of the meaning of health food. It is a book with a unique health message.

Simply defined, health food implies food that, when ingested by the human body, it will provide only health giving properties, free of digestive inhibitors, ingredients of addiction or any items not easily and readily assimilated by the healthy human organism. Consistent with this definition, a recipe book or a cook book designated 'health foods' or 'natural foods' should contain recipes comprising only healthful ingredients or those natural to human digestive capacities.

Primarily, a health food or natural food recipe book should be vegetarian. Humans are by nature, primates and their guts are designed to readily digest whole foods of plant — not animal — origin. Ingesting animal foods can be a minor difficulty for some and a debilitating problem for others.

Another essential feature of this book includes guidance to selecting and combining whole, natural foods for optimum nutritional potential. It also includes tasty, wholesome recipes that are quick to prepare without resorting to ingredients that detract from human health; ingredients that have been unquestioningly used for generations past. I refer to the use of artificial flavours such as; salt (except to control yeast), pepper, strong spices, pickles, artificial sweeteners such as cane sugar (sucrose in any form), honey, milk, butter and even margarine.

As well as avoiding the use of these common undesirable ingredients, this recipe book does not include meat, fish or fowl, yet it achieves a nutritionally sound dietary balance in its recipes. The use of cheese in some recipes will not appeal to my vegan friends, but it can easily be replaced by tofu or soya cheese to suit their dietary preferences. Otherwise, this is a definite vegetarian recipe book, with emphasis on healthy ingredients that are combined to give maximum flavour and digestive ease. Hence this book's uniqueness.

Finally, may I draw readers' attention to the fact that with around half the recipes devoted to raw foods, this is more than a cook book and I far prefer to regard it as a recipe book. In this regard, it fulfills the overlooked need of providing a wide variety of raw food dishes for the health-aware who recognise that certain nutritional losses are induced by cooking. And the time-conscious person is already aware that raw foods are nature's 'fast foods', saving valuable hours of cooking time each week.

PART ONE

HEALTHFUL NON-COOKING

When people cook food they destroy much of its nutritional value. There are, of course, methods of cooking by which losses are minimised and these I shall look at in Part Two. But the more raw foods one includes in the diet, the greater will be its nourishment and the more enjoyable its flavours.

Because raw foods are so much more nutritious than cooked, they offer greater satisfaction from smaller quantities, both to the appetite and for the body's energy and regenerative needs. There is no doubt about it, non-cooking is in every way the most satisfying diet for mankind.

As fresh fruit and vegetables occupy the bulk of man's natural diet, their preparation has to be the first consideration for any self-respecting recipe book. From years of practice and advising health-conscious people in many parts of the world, I have here brought together a selection of recipes that will delight you in every way. They are easy to prepare, delicious in flavour, high in energy and body-building nourishment, and low in cost, owing to their reliance on the seasonable availability of fresh raw fruits and vegetables.

For this reason, this book has been deliberately entitled a "recipe book", not "cook book". As half the recipes contained in it do not require any cooking at all, this book lives up to the other words on its cover — it is a health food book. Every recipe is chosen with the nutrition and health of the consumer in mind. Nearly every ingredient has some important nutritional properties that will combine well with all other ingredients in the same recipe.

Far too many recipe or cook books are now on the market with contents which do not honestly justify their titles. Far too many people are posing as experts in health and nutrition without having had both the scientific training *and* the practical experience of involvement in the health food industry. None of the contents of this book, however, will ever be false to the genuine cause of true health.

Group 1: Fruit Salads

Of all the foods given to man, fresh fruit is the easiest to eat and the highest in natural moisture and energy-producing nutrients. It is little wonder that Adam found apples so irresistible!

To many people, fresh fruit represents nothing more than a convenient snack between meals. If fresh fruits became the meal instead of the snack, their abundant nutrients would remove the unhealthy habit of snacking between meals. This not only helps avoid weight increase, but also saves on the amount of food required to properly nourish the body, as well as significantly reducing the family food bill.

Fresh fruit salads provide not only enjoyable nourishment, but they also guarantee to regulate body weight. In fact, one of the most successful and enjoyable weight-reducing diets is that comprising fresh fruit salads exclusively for a predetermined period.

For everyone, the ideal diet should include at least one raw fruit meal a day. With so many delicious fruits available and so many exciting ways to prepare them, no one need ever feel that fresh raw fruit in the diet is monotonous. Rather, it offers a blessing to one's health and total feeling of well-being such as can only derive from a fruitful life.

In selecting the following fruit salad recipes, simplicity has been the main criterion, thereby facilitating meal preparation and digestion. Nature has endowed this planet with a magnificent bounty of fresh fruits, placing at our disposal such a variety to choose from that neither our taste buds nor eyes should ever be bored. This applies even in the "slow fruit season" in temperate countries, that is, spring time. Thanks to the developments of modern transportation and storage, however, fresh fruits from far away can be made available when the off-growing season might otherwise limit the choice to citrus fruits and melons. So, with at least a dozen varieties of fruit available at any time of the year, dietary boredom is unknown.

In selecting fresh fruits for these salads, care has also been exercised to facilitate the most efficient digestion. This is achieved by taking note of food-combining rules, as outlined in my comprehensive health book, *New Dimensions in Health* (Angus & Robertson Publishers, Sydney, 1983). Correct food combinations inflict no burden on the stomach, encouraging it to speedily catabolise the small amounts of protein in fruits, so the meal soon passes into the lower intestines for the major part of its digestion. This implies that fruit meals usually pass out of the stomach more quickly than other types of meals, giving rise to that feeling of "hunger" many people experience within an hour or two of concluding a meal consisting only of fruits. This feeling only indicates that the stomach is empty and has done its job on the protein in the last meal. Take your mind off the feeling and it soon passes, allowing the duodenum and small intestine to do their catabolising without your anxiety of "starving to death". So enjoy your fresh fruit salads for their juicy flavour and their ease of digestion.

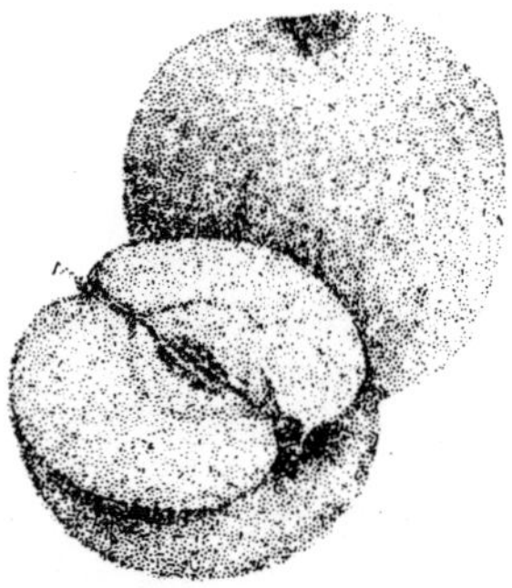

TROPICAL TREAT

With such a vast area of fruit-producing lands within the tropics, Australians are blessed with a year-round variety of fresh fruits that are both nutritious and deliciously sweet. Pawpaws and bananas are available continuously and are valuable sources of potassium, the nerve and muscle nourisher and water-retention regulator, and high-energy fructose. Mangoes are also high in potassium, as well as being excellent sources of vitamins A and C. As mangoes are only available during summer, suitable alternatives are custard apples and persimmons, both of which are fibre-rich. And custard apples are even higher in potassium than bananas. The best dates are imported from California and are similarly high in potassium, as well as in iron, niacin, fibre and fructose. This fruit salad is, therefore, ideal for active, busy people.

NO COOKING REQUIRED SERVES 2

INGREDIENTS

½ medium (or 1 small) pawpaw
1 large (or 2 small) mango
1 large (or 2 small) banana
150 g sun-dried dates

METHOD

1 Peel and dice the fresh fruit.
2 Remove the seeds and cut the dates into small pieces (quarters or sixths).
3 Put all the fruit in a serving bowl, mix and serve immediately.

ALTERNATIVES

1 Persimmons or custard apple instead of mango.
2 Raisins, sultanas or diced sun-dried figs instead of dates.

TO SERVE

This is an ideal midday meal for busy people. Prepare it only as required and do not refrigerate (to avoid oxidation and discolouration).

SWEET FRUIT SALAD

This is another quick, high-energy fresh fruit salad for the busy person. It relies more on temperate than tropical fruits, especially those available throughout the year. It provides a non-fat meal, which has become a favourite for athletes and sports people of all ages. Although dried fruits are used in this recipe, weight-conscious people need have little concern as long as they are active; if not, they should replace the dried fruits as indicated at the end of the recipe. This fruit salad is ideal for breakfast or lunch, but it is too energising for the evening meal, unless you intend a late and exciting night.

NO COOKING REQUIRED — SERVES 2

INGREDIENTS

1 large apple, cored and diced
1 large pear, cored and diced
1 large banana, peeled and sliced
1 small pawpaw, peeled, seeded and diced
8 apricots (fresh or sun-dried), pitted and diced
10 dates (fresh or sun-dried), pitted and diced
handful seedless raisins or sultanas

METHOD

1 Put prepared ingredients in bowl and lightly mix.
2 Serve immediately, as fresh fruit begins to oxidise when left standing and bananas become mushy.

ALTERNATIVES

1 Dried fruits can be replaced by any other fruit, as long as acid fruits (citrus, pineapple, passionfruit, strawberries) are not chosen, for they do not combine well with sweet fruit.
2 Fresh figs, persimmons or custard apples can be used instead of dried fruits or any other listed fruit not readily available or desired.

TO SERVE

This fruit salad is delicious served alone, but a topping of Penguin Ice Cream (page 97) will make it even more delectable and certainly richer.

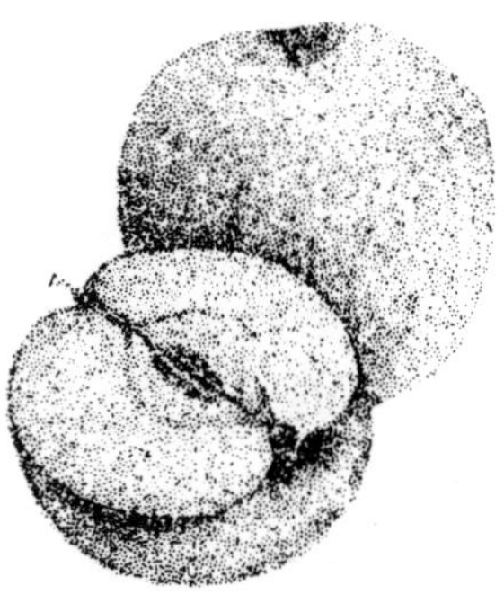

Opposite top: Melon Ball Fruit Salad (see page 5).
Opposite bottom: Low Calorie Fruit and Yoghurt Salad (see page 7).

MELON BALL FRUIT SALAD

Although rather low in nutritional value, the melon family offers a delicious variety of easily digested fruits. Owing to their high sugar (fructose) content in relation to their starch and fibre, melons rate as the most easily digested of all foods, as long as they are not included in the same meal as other foods. Ideally, melons should be eaten on their own, but for those whose stomachs can handle a variety of fruits with melons, the following recipe has been devised to provide the most appealing fruit salad, yet maintaining a simplicity such that digestive ease is not impaired.

NO COOKING REQUIRED MELON-BALLER IS NEEDED SERVES 4

INGREDIENTS

¼ long or ½ round variety watermelon
1 medium cantaloupe (rockmelon)
1 medium honeydew melon
250 g grapes, any variety, preferably seedless
250 g cherries, preferably darkest variety

METHOD

1 Use a melon-baller to extract the flesh from melons in shape of balls up to 2 cm in diameter.
2 Destalk and wash the grapes and cherries.
3 Mix all ingredients in a large serving bowl.

ALTERNATIVES

It is difficult to suggest any alternatives that are ideally suited to replacing any of these ingredients not in season. As some of the melons have a rather short season, it is better to omit one or two ingredients rather than replace them with other fruit that might not combine well and might create some digestive problems.

TO SERVE

This fruit salad tastes most appealing when served from the refrigerator. Remember, it is a meal in itself, not a dessert.

Opposite: Pawpaw Fruit Bowl (see page 8).

LOW CALORIE FRUIT AND CHEESE SALAD

For the weight-conscious person, hitherto concerned that fruit might be fattening, here is delicious proof to the contrary. In fact, a diet of only fresh fruit for a few consecutive days is a proven and reliable way to *lose* weight. This fruit salad contains only 1423 kilojoules (340 calories) in each recommended serving; by dividing the total quantity among six people, the reduced calorie count becomes 1017 kilojoules (243 calories). Ricotta or cottage cheeses are chosen for their low kilojoule content, high protein content and digestibility.

NO COOKING REQUIRED SERVES 4

INGREDIENTS
1 small (or ½ large) pineapple, peeled and cored
2 peaches, peeled and pitted
2 mangoes, peeled
2 pears, peeled and cored
2 oranges, peeled
1 small (or ½ large) pawpaw, peeled and seeded
350 g ricotta or cottage cheese

METHOD
1 Dice all fruit and put it in a suitable bowl.
2 Add cheese, which should also be chopped, and mix lightly.

ALTERNATIVES
1 Any alternative fruits can be chosen as long as they are not sweet, such as bananas, melons, or similar.
2 A similar quantity of raw nuts (ground, chopped or whole) can be used instead of cheese, but this increases kilojoules. This is, however, no problem for active people.

TO SERVE
This is a high-protein meal that also provides ample vitamins and minerals, so it should be served for lunch or the evening meal, rather than breakfast. It is often regarded as most delicious when served cold from the refrigerator.

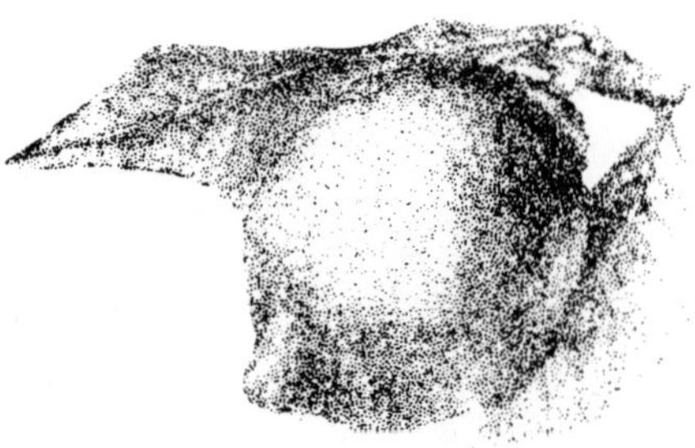

LOW CALORIE FRUIT AND YOGHURT SALAD

Continuing the theme that a suitably chosen fruit meal will be a great help to those seeking to lose weight, this low-calorie fruit salad provides added variety to the diet of the weight-conscious person. This recipe is even slightly lower in kilojoules than the previous one, but it is also lower in protein owing to the use of yoghurt rather than cheese.

NO COOKING REQUIRED SERVES 4

INGREDIENTS

1 small pineapple
1 large apple
2 kiwifruit (Chinese gooseberries)
2 grapefruit, peeled
2 mandarins, peeled
200–250 g goat's milk yoghurt

METHOD

1 Cut the skin from pineapple; cut the flesh into rings and dice, removing the core.
2 Remove the core from the apple, peel if desired, and dice.
3 Peel the kiwifruit and slice laterally about 2 mm thick.
4 Break the grapefruit and mandarins into segments.
5 Mix all the fruit, except the kiwifruit, in a large bowl.
6 Decorate the top of the fruit salad with the slices of kiwifruit.

ALTERNATIVES

1 In place of any of the recommended fruits, orange and pear can be used.
2 If goat's milk yoghurt is not available, use cow's milk variety with the fewest undesirable additives (sweeteners, artificial setting agents, and preservatives are often used). The best yoghurt is the one you make at home from raw milk, preferably goat's.

TO SERVE

As apple and pear oxidise quickly, prepare this fruit salad only when it is to be eaten. If it has to be stored for any length of time, keep it in the refrigerator and ensure that the dish is tightly covered.

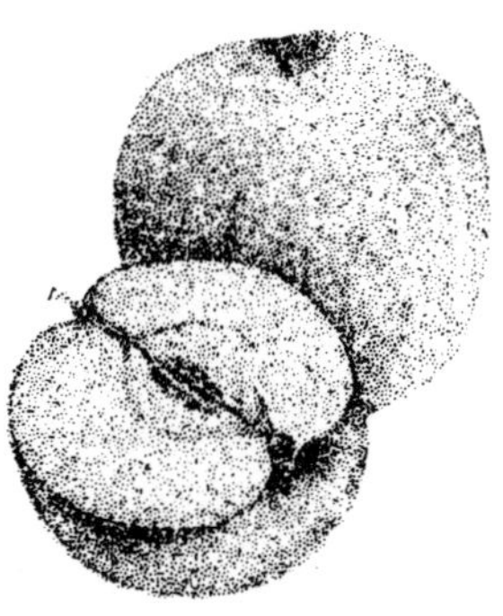

PAWPAW FRUIT BOWL

In terms of general nutritional properties, the pawpaw is around the top of the fruit list. It is 28 per cent richer in vitamin C than oranges, as well as being an excellent fruit source of vitamin A and potassium. The vitamin C content of pawpaw means it combines well with nuts, helping the body to digest their protein richness. This is, indeed, a protein-rich fruit salad, which uses the convenient shape of the pawpaw as the bowl in which the ingredients are gathered and served.

NO COOKING REQUIRED SERVES 2

INGREDIENTS

1 large pawpaw (½ per person)
½ punnet strawberries
2 fresh apricots or peaches
100 g raw cashew nuts
80 g raw brazil nut kernels
2 passionfruit

METHOD

1 Cut the pawpaw in half and remove the seeds.
2 Cut the strawberries in halves and put them in the pawpaw halves.
3 Slice the apricots or peaches and put them in the pawpaw halves.
4 Add the nuts and passionfruit and mix them inside each pawpaw half.

ALTERNATIVES

1 If stone fruit is out of season, pears or a pineapple can be used.
2 Strawberries or passionfruit can be replaced by two kiwifruit or by a segmented orange or two mandarins.
3 Brazil nuts can be replaced by hazelnuts or almond kernels. If using almonds, buy "naturals" (with the skin on) rather than blanched ones, which have been chemically skinned. To remove skins, stand the almonds in boiling water for a minute, then rinse in cold water; the skin then swells and is easily squeezed off.
4 Instead of using whole nut kernels in the recipe, they can be ground into a coarse meal or cut into chunks for easier mixing.

TO SERVE

This recipe is too rich for breakfast, so should be served for lunch or the evening meal. It is especially beneficial for busy people, because it requires little preparation and almost no washing up. This recipe can also be prepared ahead of time and placed in the refrigerator, as long as it is well covered to minimise oxidation.

HIGH-FIBRE FRUIT SALAD

Pecan and macadamia nuts are exceptions in the nut domain. While other nuts are classified as protein concentrates, these are low in protein but exceptionally high in fibre and in natural unsaturated fats. All nuts possess high concentrations of fat, but these two contain more than 70 per cent fat by weight. Be not deterred, however, as unsaturated fats are essential to ideal body functioning. In this recipe, the nuts are combined with fruits that will help their metabolism, for they are fruits with the highest offering of vitamin C — guavas, pawpaws, and strawberries. In fact, guavas contain more than five times the vitamin C of oranges; they are also high in alkalising minerals and niacin, and especially rich in dietary fibre — richer than any other fresh food.

NO COOKING REQUIRED — SERVES 4

INGREDIENTS

4 guavas, peeled
1 punnet (250 g) strawberries
2 oranges, peeled
2 kiwifruit, peeled
1 small (or ½ large) pawpaw, peeled and seeded
400 g pecan nut kernels

METHOD

1 Dice all the fruit into a suitable size for mixing.
2 Chop the nuts into small pieces or grind them into a coarse meal.
3 Mix all the ingredients in a large serving bowl.

ALTERNATIVES

1 Raw macadamia nut kernels can replace pecans, or a mixture of both can be used for additional variety. Do not exceed a total quantity of about 400 g.
2 As guavas only have a short season in temperate climates (they are tropical fruits which grow wild in jungles), use them abundantly when they are available during their summer. When they are out of season, replace them with grapefruit, mandarins, or increase the quantity of one or two of the existing ingredients.

TO SERVE

This fruit salad is very chewy, especially when guavas are used. It is not a meal to be rushed; allow plenty of chewing time and get maximum enjoyment of the salad's delicious flavours. When guavas are used, it is an especially fibre-rich meal, making it ideal for anyone suffering from constipation.

Group 2: Vegetable Salads

Every New Age nutritionist knows that man's staple food is the raw vegetable salad. It is so far ahead of any other meal as the most flavoursome and highly nutritious that its place in the daily menu should be unquestioned. "Give us this day our daily salad" should be our morning prayer, for without the inclusion of the vegetable salad in the day's menu, we are depriving ourselves of optimum nutriments, which must, in turn, impair our body's efficiency.

No meal can be prepared more speedily than the simple salad. Salads with special varieties in appearance or flavour, however, require a little more time and care. Yet a salad, no matter how involved it may become, will never occupy even half the time demanded by the preparation of a baked, roasted, grilled, or fried main course. And the time required by the body to digest a raw vegetable salad, if properly chewed, is less than half that demanded by the alternatives. Another bonus is that the proportional increase in nutriments offered by the salad is more than double that possible from a cooked meal, especially if it is baked, fried or stewed.

An almost limitless variety of salad vegetables is available throughout most of the year in almost every country of the world. The more temperate the country's climate, the greater the variety. In countries where months of excessive heat or extreme cold prevail, local supplies of fresh salad vegetables tend to diminish. But with today's modern and rapid systems of transportation, the products of the temperate zones are speedily (often within hours of being picked and packed) brought to less climatically fortunate areas.

To supplement the supply of freshly produced farm crops of salad vegetables, there is the glorious pleasure of producing your own food crop. If your home is blessed with a garden no problems exist. Alternatively, the European idea of renting or owning a small plot of arable land outside the city for cultivation of the family's needs during weekends is a desirable concept. In any case, the kitchen is an ideal spot for the production of part of the family's salad requirements using the system of sprouting.

Most people, certainly many New Age mothers, understand the method of sprouting and the tremendous nutritional properties and delicious flavours available from sprouted foods. Sprouting is briefly described below.

Alfalfa seeds, mung beans (Chinese bean sprouts), brown lentils, wheat, sunflower seeds, and green soya beans are among the dried foods that lend themselves to sprouting and to the dynamic increase in nutrients provided by the four or five day growth. Sprouting not only provides the most nutritious components for the raw vegetable salad, but also offers the cheapest source of ingredients. In fact, all ingredients in the raw vegetable salad are far less expensive (even if they have to be flown in by jet plane) than cuts of tender animal meats and their preparation and cooking, and less expensive than canned or preserved "convenience foods", most of which offer so little in the way of cellular nourishment that you are often better discarding the contents and eating the package!

I have heard some people remark that a bunch of celery in Brisbane, especially if organically grown, can cost up to $2.50 in winter if it has been freighted from Adelaide. "This is too much," they say. Yet these same people have no qualms about spending far more than that on a can of Alaskan salmon or crab meat. The same remarks hold when an avocado, costing about $1.50, is compared with a pound of T-bone steak: the avocado might weigh only a third as much as the steak, yet it contains nearly as much usable protein, only a quarter the fat, infinitely more dietary fibre and vitamin C (meat has none of either), and thirty times as much vitamin A. An avocado weighing 150 grams has less vitamin B and minerals than meat, but most of these are reduced considerably when the meat is cooked, and others are diminished because they need to combine with some of the acids in the meat to avoid hyperacidity in the body.

Vegetable salads may vary from the simple finger salad, in which the ingredients are retained in the whole state and eaten *au naturel*, to the highly colourful and complex ones that are possible if you wish to create a special impression. Some of this extensive range is offered in the following pages including a few steamed vegetables as optional extras, for those who seek added variety or are encumbered by false teeth, which inhibit proper chewing.

An infinite variety of dressings may be used with raw vegetable salads for added flavouring. Commercial ones are generally offered in powdered or liquid form and are invariably based on salt, spices, herbs, or oils. Better dressings are always those made yourself, and a great range of foods can be employed. Many of these are suggested in this section.

Common salt and strong herbs and spices should be avoided as these are detrimental to the gastrointestinal tract and are recognised digestive inhibitors. Their association with digestive disorders and many of the body's cellular diseases has been conclusively proven. It is far better to use only a dash of vegetable seasoning free from added spices or salt.

If you wish to use prepared dressings based on oils, such as mayonnaise or merely particular vegetable oils, it is wise to buy only those made from cold-pressing extraction methods, usually termed "cold-pressed". This indicates that the oils have been extracted by expeller presses and have been kept free from solvent chemicals used in the large-scale extraction of commercial oils. The chemical solvent (usually hexane) used to dissolve the oil can never be guaranteed to be completely evaporated from the mixture — only one of the many reasons why chemically extracted oils are cheaper, less desirable, and potentially dangerous when used for human consumption.

Similarly, when buying a mayonnaise, select only brands that guarantee freedom from hydrogenation. The primary advantage of vegetable oils is their high concentration of polyunsaturated fatty acids, but when they are hydrogenised, saturation of the oils takes place, rendering them more difficult to digest and unsuitable for the system. Good quality cold-pressed vegetable oils and mayonnaises are generally available only from health food stores.

Tossed Salads

The basic ingredients for tossed salads are raw vegetables. For added variety, steamed vegetables can also be used, but it is preferable to use raw wherever possible. The preparation of standard tossed salads involves some techniques to minimise oxidation losses in the vitamin content of many vegetables. Vitamin A is especially susceptible to decrease from oxidation. It is important to use only those vegetables in season, always avoiding canned or frozen vegetables — and choosing the freshest, the best.

Lettuce. The basis of any salad, it should be torn into suitably sized pieces. Tears generally should follow veins in the leaf, as shredding exposes more surface to rapid oxidation.

Celery. Slice each stick into suitable pieces, using leaves for added flavour and nutrients.

Carrot. Grate carrot coarsely rather than finely, preferably with a stainless steel grater. If the carrot is intended for a starch salad, a light sprinkling with cold-pressed oil will help suspend oxidation; toss grated carrot well by itself so that the oil can cover most of the exposed surfaces. Alternatively, lightly steam carrots and cut into rings or into diced pieces.

Beetroot. This can be treated in the same way as carrot, either grated or steamed.

Capsicums. Cut these into strips or diced pieces for tossing in a salad. Some strips can be used to decorate the top of the salad just before serving. Skins can be removed by fine paring for anyone with chewing or digestive difficulties.

Cucumbers. Use cucumbers with the skin retained and cut into sliced rings; cut each ring into two or four segments if preferred smaller. Remove the skin if it is tough or if there is any risk of indigestion for people who cannot chew sufficiently well. Do not scrape the outer surfaces when the skins have been removed — this increases oxidation, with no known advantage.

Cabbage. This can be served shredded or grated, but the larger the pieces, the less the oxidation loss. Cabbage can be lightly steamed before shredding if preferred, but it will then be less nutritious.

Cauliflower. This can be enjoyed raw by cutting away from the stalks and breaking into small flowerets. Alternatively, it can be lightly steamed and then cut into pieces of suitable size.

Zucchini. Cut into thin slices for use raw, or steam lightly, then slice into thicker rings.

Peas. These can be removed from their pods and used raw if they are young and tender. Otherwise, lightly steam; flavour is retained better if steamed in pods.

String beans. Slice and use raw, or lightly steam them and cut into larger pieces; remove strings only after cooking.

Tomatoes. These should be used only when the salad is to accompany a protein-rich meal. Otherwise, do not use them in a tossed salad, but serve them separately, as they have a high acid content. Allow those who prefer correct food combinations to avoid them when starches are to be eaten at the same meal. For use in a tossed salad, tomatoes can be either sliced or diced; try to retain each piece whole.

Brussels sprouts. These are best lightly steamed, then cut into halves or quarters, depending on individual sizes.

Broccoli. This can be used raw or lightly steamed and cut into suitable pieces so that each small head retains its individual shape.

When using steamed vegetables in a tossed salad, be sure they are cool before mixing them with other ingredients to avoid turning other ingredients limp.

The best type of bowl in which to mix your tossed salad is glass; next best is wooden. Avoid plastic and enamelised metal, especially aluminium. It is wise to prepare salad immediately prior to the meal; but if this is not possible, cover it as air-tight as possible as soon as it is prepared, then put it in the refrigerator. Be sure that it does not get too cold. Do not add salad dressing until ready to serve.

Tossed salads can be served either direct from the mixing bowl or placed on large lettuce leaves. In each case some colourful garnish will always add to a salad's eye appeal. Rings of tomato, capsicum (especially red), and cucumber always look good. Sprigs of broccoli flowers and leaves of celery will also add attractiveness.

Highly nutritious and delicious additions to tossed salads are the sprouted pulses, such as lentils, mung beans, alfalfa, and sunflower seeds. Alfalfa sprouts can be used in any tossed salad. It is advisable to use all others only with protein-rich meals, as their own protein concentration is significant.

For protein-rich salads, either nuts or seeds also can be used. They can be tossed with the vegetables, placed decoratively atop the salad, or served separately. Cottage or ricotta cheese can also be added to a tossed salad; so can soya cheese.

Onions, radishes, or garlic are best avoided to maintain good digestion. Some people prefer herb flavourings to garnish tossed salads, but these should be used only if they are very mild, and they should be used in small quantities, owing to their general astringent characteristics. Small sprigs of mint or parsley might be used occasionally to garnish the bowl.

Simple Sprouting

The two easiest and cheapest ways of sprouting seeds are in a mesh-covered jar, or in a trough with a stainless steel mesh insert.

The jar should be round and rest on its side. To aid in this a rack or shelf is needed near the sink on which to store it and keep it stationary. This method guarantees the sprouts being freshest, as they can be thoroughly rinsed to avoid souring.

The size of the jar is of minor consequence, since an amazingly large number of sprouts can be raised in a confined space. For the average family, one 1 litre screw-top jar with a mesh insert in the top is sufficient. The mesh may be cheesecloth, a piece of nylon stocking or, ideally, a stainless steel wire. You might need several jars to keep a good variety of sprouts constantly on hand for sandwiches, salads, casseroles, omelets, and the like.

A suitable sprouting trough can also be used. This can be of heavy gauge plastic, as long as the sprouting bed is a stainless steel wire mesh. The sprouts will grow on this mesh, but the trough must be so constructed that the mesh is supported by a ridge about 1 centimetre above the base of the trough.

Favourite seeds to sprout are alfalfa and mung bean, but many people now also enjoy brown lentils and green soya beans (the common dry variety does not sprout well). Make sure the seed, pulse or grain you wish to grow has not been treated or processed so as to inhibit growth. Do not sprout seeds commercially prepared for planting.

These are the steps generally followed.

1. Presoak 1 or 2 tablespoons of seeds overnight in water as pure as you can obtain.
2. Rinse under tap (in colander or strainer if using sprouting tray). Drain.
3. If using a trough, distribute the seeds evenly over the wire mesh, or if an enclosed sprouter, evenly over the sprouting bed. If sprouting in a jar, be sure to tilt the jar towards its opening so that any excess water will come forward, away from the sprouts.
4. Whichever method is being used, place the container in a dark area, such as a cupboard or pantry, for about 12 hours.
5. Bring the jar or tray out into the light, but not into direct sunlight. Place it near the sink for ease of rinsing (jar), or sprinkling (tray) which must be done twice a day (three times a day if you live in a dry climate).
6. You will be able to enjoy your sprouts within four or five days of the initial soaking period. Watch for green tips to appear. The height of the sprouts will vary according to the variety. The important guide is the appearance of the green at the ends. When these appear the sprouts are ready for eating and are at their most succulent.

Sprouts add a lovely juiciness to every dish to which you choose to add them, but do not cook them. Wait until the cooked dish is ready for eating, then add the sprouts. This will heat them just long enough to warm them.

In tossed salads, add any amount of sprouts according to your taste, but not until the last minute, so that they are neither bruised nor broken when the salad is tossed. Let them remain whole and see how delightfully tempting they make the salad appear and taste.

NATURAL FINGER SALAD

Before the advent of cutlery and crockery, pristine man ate food with a natural enthusiasm that rarely appears at today's sophisticated dining table. Perhaps we are too concerned with how to eat and too unconcerned with what and when to eat. What to eat is best satisfied by fresh salad vegetables served whole; when to eat is best determined by the empty stomach. So when next you are drawn to opening your refrigerator door by the cries of your empty stomach, reach for the following ingredients and enjoy them from your fingers, *au naturel.*

NO COOKING REQUIRED SERVES 2

INGREDIENTS

4 large lettuce leaves, left whole
2 medium tomatoes, left whole
1 medium cucumber, cut in half
2 stalks celery, uncut
1 capsicum, cut in half and cored
4 small carrots, left whole
1 large avocado, cut in half and seeded
1 cup fresh lentil sprouts

METHOD

1 Clean all the vegetables under running water.
2 Leave the skins on all vegetables and arrange on two platters.
3 Serve immediately to avoid nutritional and flavour losses from oxidation or heat.

ALTERNATIVES

1 Instead of avocado, 180 g raw unsalted nuts (almonds, Brazils, cashews or hazels) or 130 g raw unsalted sunflower or pumpkin seed kernels can be used to change this salad into a protein-concentrate meal.
2 Other vegetables in season can be substituted; always choose the crispest and freshest available. If growing your own vegetables, use more of these and reduce the variety.
3 The salad should always include fresh sprouts; choose from alfalfa, mung bean or any other variety instead of lentils if desired.

TO SERVE

Any one of the variety of dips, dressings or mayonnaise, for which recipes are given later, can be used with this salad. But choose any garnish to accord with basic food combining rules for best digestion (e.g. do not use a cheese dressing with nuts).

ANTI-ARTHRITIC AVOCADO SALAD

For those who enjoy the taste kaleidoscope of delicious salad vegetables tossed together but must avoid acid-forming foods, this meal is a winner. It is an all-vegetable salad, with avocado forming the nutritional centrepiece. Contrary to popular opinion, avocado is not fattening, for it is lower in kilojoules than meat, fish or chicken, as well as being devoid of uric acid, a precursor to arthritis. Avocado is probably the most nutritious fruit known to man, and it combines perfectly with salad vegetables for nutritional and taste delectability. With the addition of alfalfa sprouts, this salad becomes even more alkalising, an important anti-arthritic property of food.

NO COOKING REQUIRED SERVES 4

INGREDIENTS

2 medium carrots
2 tablespoons fresh lemon juice
2 stalks celery, chopped
1 large cucumber, sliced
1 red capsicum, cored and diced
100 g raw mushrooms, diced
2 cups alfalfa sprouts
2 large avocados, peeled and sliced

METHOD

1 Scrub and grate the carrots, then toss them in lemon juice.
2 Mix all the vegetables, except avocado, in a large serving bowl.
3 Decorate the top of the salad with sliced avocado and serve.

ALTERNATIVES

If steamed vegetables are desired for variety, green beans, fresh peas, broccoli, Brussels sprouts, and so on, can be used as additions or alternatives. Steam them only until just tender and do not add them to the salad mixture until they have cooled.

TO SERVE

This is an ideal salad for anyone, whether arthritic or not. It is perfect for a midday or evening meal, or it can be made in half the quantity and served as a side salad with a main meal.

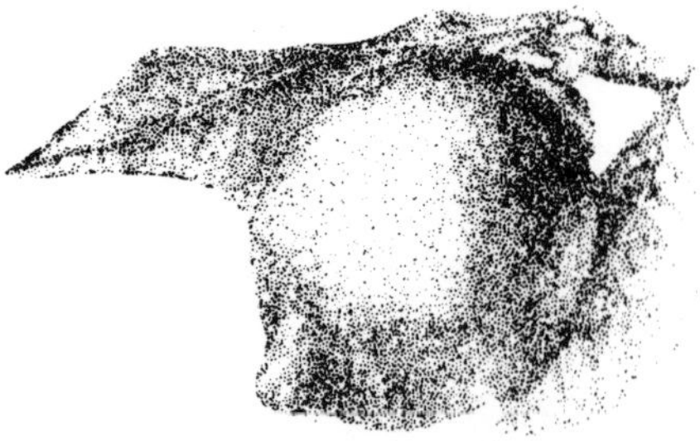

SWISS CHEESE SALAD

Probably no type of salad has greater universality of appeal than a cheese salad. No matter where one travels throughout the world, no matter in what type of restaurant one chooses to dine, or on what airline one travels, there is always an excellent chance of obtaining a reasonable cheese salad. But, what variations in cheeses there are! As block cheeses are the most convenient to keep and serve, this salad has been selected to illustrate just how delicious and nutritious a cheese salad can be. And the most desirable cheese to satisfy these demands is genuine Swiss Emmenthaler. Cultured only from whole milk (usually raw and from alpine pastures), Swiss Emmenthaler is recognised by its characteristic nut-sweet flavour and smooth, oily texture. For block cheese, it has an exceptionally low salt content, and it is further characterised by its many round holes throughout the block. Swiss inspectors maintain strict standards on this, one of the most difficult cheeses to make, for no artificial additives or colourings are permitted. Nutritionally, it is a superior cheese, with the highest calcium content of any cheese (almost 1 per cent by weight), an excellent calcium–phosphorus ratio, and the highest protein level to be found in cheese (28.8 per cent). But it must be genuine Swiss Emmenthaler.

NO COOKING REQUIRED — SERVES 4

INGREDIENTS

400 g Swiss Emmenthaler cheese, cut into cubes
2 medium tomatoes, cut into chunks
2 stalks celery including tops, chopped
1 cucumber, sliced
1/3 cup parsley, chopped
1 red capsicum, cored and diced
1 raw beetroot, scrubbed and grated
1 cup alfalfa sprouts

METHOD
Simply mix all the ingredients in a large serving bowl.

ALTERNATIVES
1 Ricotta or cottage cheese can be used instead of Swiss.
2 If locally made block cheeses are preferred for convenience or economy, choose only those with low salt and mild texture for best digestive and health properties.

TO SERVE
This salad is a complete, nutritious meal and is ideal for the midday or evening banquet. If you want added dressing, try fresh lemon juice or Instant Fresh Mayonnaise (page 30).

SUNFLOWER SESAME SALAD

This is both a highly nutritious and a relatively inexpensive salad. It is a protein-rich meal that uses two of the most economical sources of primary quality protein available: sunflower seed kernels and sesame seeds. Both of these are readily available from health food stores at prices less than top cuts of meat, yet they have far greater nutritional properties. Both are also far richer than meat in vital fibre and polyunsaturated fats. For variety, lightly steamed vegetables are used here, an aspect of versatile salad making that is often overlooked.

LIGHT STEAMING ONLY OF SOME INGREDIENTS SERVES 4

INGREDIENTS

1 cup fresh broccoli flowerets
1 cup fresh cauliflower flowerets
125 g raw sunflower seed kernels
125 g raw tahini paste (sesame butter)
2 stalks celery, chopped
1 red capsicum, cored and diced
½ cup fresh lentil sprouts
⅓ cup parsley, chopped
½ cup fresh cabbage, shredded

METHOD

1 Scrub all the vegetables.
2 Lightly steam the broccoli and cauliflower (see page 12).
3 Grind the sunflower seeds into a coarse meal, using a nut or coffee grinder, a blender or a hand mill.
4 Mix the sunflower meal into the tahini to make a thick paste.
5 As soon as the steamed vegetables have cooled, mix them with the other vegetables in a large serving bowl.
6 Pour the sunflower–tahini paste over the mixture and either leave it on top or mix it in lightly.

ALTERNATIVES

1 Raw pumpkin seed kernels (pepitas) are an ideal alternative to sunflower seeds; they are more expensive, but they are richer in protein, phosphorus, and iron.
2 Mung bean sprouts can be used instead of lentils, but avoid alfalfa sprouts in this salad, as they do not mix well with cooked vegetables, because they become limp and soggy.
3 Substitute any vegetables not in season with any that are, but try to retain similar types.

TO SERVE

This is a full meal and needs no supplementing, other than with a small glass of fresh carrot juice if you feel thirsty.

SEED AND SPROUT SALAD

This is a variation to the previous Sunflower Sesame Salad, but it concentrates on pepitas, rather than using tahini. It is, therefore, designed as a high-protein salad, for pepitas are the richest sources of protein food readily available for human consumption. With 29 per cent protein, they contain far more than all nuts (except pignolia kernels, which are often difficult to obtain fresh) and soya beans (34 per cent in dry state, but they cannot be eaten without much cooking, which reduces the usable protein). This salad also uses two varieties of fresh sprouts and mushrooms and avocados, further valuable sources of protein, minerals, and vitamins.

NO COOKING REQUIRED SERVES 4

INGREDIENTS

1 large (or 2 small) avocado
200 g fresh small mushrooms
200 g pumpkin seed kernels (pepitas)
½ cup fresh alfalfa sprouts
½ cup fresh lentil sprouts
2 large tomatoes, cut into chunks
2 stalks celery, chopped
4 large lettuce leaves, torn into small pieces
1 red capsicum, cored and diced
1 raw beetroot, scrubbed and grated

METHOD

1. Peel the avocado and cut it into chunks.
2. Wash the mushrooms, remove the stalks, and cut the caps into chunks.
3. If desired, grind pepitas into a coarse meal (or leave whole if everyone has good teeth).
4. Mix all the ingredients together in a large serving bowl.

ALTERNATIVES

1. Any varieties of fresh sprouts can be used, for example, mung bean can replace lentils, and sunflower sprouts can be used for alfalfa.
2. One of the varieties of sprouts can be replaced by ½ cup chopped parsley.
3. Any vegetables not in season can be replaced with any that are, but try to keep to the same style of vegetable.
4. Sunflower or sesame seeds, or a combination of seeds, can be used instead of all the pepitas to reduce cost.
5. Any of the following raw, unsalted nuts can be used, either singly or together, instead of pepitas or other seeds (almonds, cashews, Brazils, hazelnuts, walnuts). Use them either whole or ground. These provide an interesting flavour variation, but as they are lower in protein, more are required (300–350 g in total).

VARIEGATED SUMMER SALAD

Another high-protein salad, this variation has particular advantages in summer. It is best prepared well in advance of the meal to allow adequate time for refrigeration (be careful to avoid freezing it). Almonds are used here as the primary source of protein, for they are regarded nutritionally as the number one nut and, as they are most alkaline, they are also ideal for arthritis and hyper-acidity sufferers. A small amount of cooking is needed for this recipe, which makes it an attractive presentation for the centre of your table at mealtime.

ALL RAW, EXCEPT FOR STEAMING PUMPKIN — SERVES 6

INGREDIENTS

250 g butternut pumpkin
4 tablespoons raw tahini (sesame butter)
1 large tomato, diced finely
250 g blanched almond pieces
250 g raw cashew nut pieces
250 g fresh mushrooms, chopped finely
2 stalks celery, chopped finely
1 red capsicum, cored and diced finely
1 long thin green cucumber, sliced thinly

METHOD

1 Steam the pumpkin until it is tender, then mash it thoroughly.
2 Mix the tahini, tomato and pumpkin together and mash thoroughly.
3 Add the nuts, mushrooms, celery and capsicum to this mixture and again mix thoroughly.
4 Line the inside of a bowl (desirably glass) as thoroughly as possible with sliced cucumber.
5 Place the mixture into bowl and press it down firmly.
6 Refrigerate until it is thoroughly cold.

ALTERNATIVES

1 Walnut pieces or pine nuts can be used instead of cashew nuts.
2 Raw zucchinis can be used instead of cucumber for inside the bowl.
3 Any other variety of pumpkin can be used instead of butternut, although butternut has the sweetest flavour of any pumpkin.
4 Any of the salad dressings described below can be used instead of tahini.

TO SERVE

This salad should be eased out of the bowl like a firm jelly from a mould. Then place it in the centre of the table and surround it with a variety of other vegetables, such as lightly steamed asparagus spears, green beans, brussels sprouts, plus fresh raw vegetables such as sprouts, grated carrot and beetroot, and top it with sprigs of parsley.

Opposite: Swiss Cheese Salad (see page 17).

TOSSED NUT SALAD

For those who recognise and enjoy the flavoursome, protein-rich versatility of raw, unsalted nuts, this tossed salad will become a favourite. It offers an exceptionally wide variety of flavours from the various combinations of nuts chosen to accompany a similarly diverse range of fresh vegetables. Many people who enjoy the flavour of nuts are reluctant to eat them because they fear the fat content. But the fats contained in nuts are mostly the essential fatty acids of oleic and linoleic acids. Certainly nuts are high in fats, but these are not the heart-affecting saturated fats so prolific in animal meats and products. Walnuts, for instance, are exceptionally high sources of polyunsaturated linoleic acid. You should, however, be aware of the flavour differences between Californian and Asian (Indian and Chinese) walnuts: Californian are discernibly sweeter and lighter in colour.

NO COOKING REQUIRED SERVES 4

INGREDIENTS

½ small head of lettuce
125 g raw cashew nut pieces
125 g raw walnut pieces
125 g raw pine nut kernels
1 cup fresh alfalfa sprouts
1 raw beetroot, grated
2 medium tomatoes, cored and diced
⅓ cup parsley, chopped
1 cup fresh cauliflower flowerets
2 stalks celery, chopped
1 green capsicum, cored and diced

METHOD

1 Separate lettuce leaves and tear them into smaller pieces.
2 Place all the ingredients into a large serving bowl and toss thoroughly.

ALTERNATIVES

1 Almost any combination of nuts can be used, but if the larger kernels are chosen, it is best to chop them into smaller pieces.
2 Lentil or mung bean sprouts can be used instead of alfalfa.
3 Broccoli flowerets can be used instead of cauliflower.
4 Raw cabbage can be used instead of lettuce.
5 If additional flavour is required, add a tablespoon of Instant Fresh Mayonnaise (page 30) before tossing the salad.

TO SERVE

This salad is a complete meal in these proportions. Smaller servings can be served as a side salad to steamed vegetables if desired (in which case this recipe could serve six or more people).

Opposite top: Anti-Arthritic Avocado Salad (see page 16).
Opposite bottom: Carrot and Raisin Salad (see page 26).

MEDITERRANEAN TOSSED SALAD

This is essentially a savoury salad featuring many ingredients indigenous to countries surrounding the Mediterranean Sea. It is a protein-concentrate meal using ricotta cheese (an Italian derived, whey-based, fresh cheese) as the nutritional focus, complemented by olives, olive oil, and steamed zucchinis for a delightful flavour base. A few pine nut kernels are also used for their very pleasant texture, additional flavour, and protein value (they originated in France and Italy but are now grown extensively throughout the Mediterranean region).

NO COOKING REQUIRED SERVES 4

INGREDIENTS

150 g small fresh mushrooms, cut in halves
½ small red cabbage
375 g fresh ricotta cheese
2 tablespoons cold-pressed olive oil
125 g raw pine nut kernels
125 g drained black olives
8 small, fresh zucchinis, sliced thinly
⅓ cup parsley, chopped
2 stalks celery, chopped
1 green capsicum, cored and diced

METHOD

1 Wash the mushrooms, remove cores (if desired), and cut or slice.
2 Wash the cabbage, remove any coarse outer leaves, then finely shred.
3 Chop the cheese into 1 cm cubes.
4 Smear a little of the olive oil around the inside of a large (preferably wooden) serving bowl.
5 Place all solid ingredients in the bowl, sprinkle olive oil on top, and mix thoroughly until salad is completely tossed.

ALTERNATIVES

1 Pistachio nut pieces can be used instead of pine nuts.
2 If red cabbage is unavailable, use ordinary cabbage or lettuce.
3 Sesame oil or other cold-pressed salad oil can be used instead of olive oil.
4 For additional flavour a few capers can be sprinkled over the salad when it has been tossed; a salt-free vegetable seasoning powder (such as Dr Jensen's Seasoning) can also be lightly sprinkled before tossing. Added seasoning should be used carefully to avoid overly stimulating the appetite, which may result in over-eating.

TO SERVE

This salad is a complete meal when served in large portions as suggested here. Smaller portions can be served as side salads.

MEXICAN MAYONNAISE

Contrary to the reputation of Mexican food, this is a mildly savoury salad, containing none of the spicy, heat-inducing ingredients relished as vital appetite stimulants by some people. Nutritional research suggests that hot peppers and chillis should be avoided, like the curries of Asia, as these condiments are digestive irritants that often cause gastric ulceration. The skilful combination of salad ingredients for optimum digestion and taste appreciation is the art of a good chef.

ALL INGREDIENTS RAW, EXCEPT CORN AND PEAS SERVES 4

INGREDIENTS
4 cobs young sweet corn
400 g fresh green peas in pods
2 medium carrots, scrubbed and grated
1 raw young beetroot, scrubbed and grated
150 g small fresh mushrooms, cut in halves
½ cup fresh mung bean or lentil sprouts
2 stalks celery, chopped
1 red or green capsicum, cored and diced
1 tablespoon Instant Fresh Mayonnaise (page 30)
1 medium avocado, peeled and cut in wedges

METHOD
1 Steam the corn cobs until just tender.
2 Steam the peas whole until the pods and peas are tender. (This ensures maximum flavour and nutrient retention.)
3 Gently cut corn kernels from the cobs so that the corn germ (pointed end of kernel attaching to cob) also comes away.
4 Remove the peas from the pods and put in a large serving bowl.
5 Add all the other ingredients to the bowl, except the avocado, and mix thoroughly.
6 Decorate the top of the salad with avocado wedges.

ALTERNATIVES
1 If young snow peas are available, they can be used instead of pod peas, in which case they are steamed and served whole in the salad, or cut into halves or smaller pieces with scissors, if desired.
2 Instead of mayonnaise, tahini can be used to provide a flavour variation and additional protein.
3 Thinly sliced raw zucchini can also be used in addition to or instead of any other vegetable not readily available.

TO SERVE
This salad contains modest amounts, rather than high concentrations, of any major nutrient, allowing its versatile use in smaller servings as a side salad for almost any meal. When served in the quantities indicated in this recipe, it should be regarded as a carbohydrate/fat meal, with high fibre content.

SAVOURY POTATO SALAD

The humble potato has for too long been the victim of misconceptions about its carbohydrate and kilojoule content. Nutritionally, potatoes are classified as carbohydrate (starch) foods, but this does not imply they are "fattening" (unless they are fried and eaten in excessive quantities — but almost any food is fattening under those conditions). Potatoes contain 80 per cent water and 17 per cent carbohydrate, so their kilojoule count is a mere 320 per 100 grams. They have a lower carbohydrate content than bananas, figs, rice, lentils and bread, and a lower kilojoule count than eggs, tuna, chicken, meat and all cheeses. As highly alkalising foods, potatoes are among the most nutritious of vegetables, as are sweet potatoes. Ideally, potatoes should be steamed, as in this salad, where they are combined to form a colourful, flavoursome and most tempting version of the ever-popular potato salad.

ALL INGREDIENTS RAW, EXCEPT FOR STEAMED POTATOES SERVES 4

INGREDIENTS

500 g fresh potatoes
250 g sweet potatoes (yellow or orange varieties preferred)
sprinkling of cold-pressed vegetable oil
2 medium carrots, grated
sprinkling of cold-pressed Italian or herb dressing
1 green cucumber, halved lengthways and sliced
1 green capsicum, cored and diced
½ cup fresh lentil or mung bean sprouts
150 g fresh mushrooms, diced
2 stalks celery, chopped
1 medium avocado

METHOD

1. Steam all potatoes until suitably tender, preferably in their jackets.
2. Dice the potatoes while still hot; put them in a mixing bowl and sprinkle with oil.
3. Wash and grate the carrots, add to potatoes, and lightly sprinkle with oil and mix them together.
4. Sprinkle sufficient dressing into a serving bowl to cover the inside of the bowl.
5. Put cucumber, capsicum, sprouts, mushrooms and celery in serving bowl; sprinkle with more dressing and toss together.
6. Add potatoes and carrot to serving bowl and mix together.
7. Peel and slice the avocado and arrange on top of mixed salad.

ALTERNATIVES

1. Sweet potato can be replaced by pumpkin or sweet corn cut from the cob.
2. A fresh, grated beetroot can be added for additional flavour and colour.
3. A few torn lettuce leaves can be added, but only when the salad is completely cool.
4. Mayonnaise or another type of salad dressing can be added; choose from those on pages 27 to 30.
5. Steamed and sliced zucchini can be used instead of cucumber.
6. Steamed green peas or beans can be used instead of capsicum.

TO SERVE

This salad can be prepared in advance and refrigerated, as the oils and dressing will effectively minimise oxidation. A bed of fresh, large lettuce leaves can provide an attractive serving base for this salad. It can be accompanied by suitable bread, such as Indian Corn Chapati (page 85), spread with avocado and/or tahini (avocado and tahini mashed together is delicious spread on bread), or spread with a raw nut butter.

COOKING TIPS

Potatoes. Optimum nutrient and flavour retention occur when potatoes are steamed in their skins until just soft enough to be pierced with a sharp fork. Ensure they are thoroughly scrubbed clean beforehand.

Sweet corn. Always steam corn whole until the kernels are soft enough to pull off the cob. When kernels are to be removed for a salad, such as this, they will come away from the cob complete with their "germ", the end by which they are attached to the cob. If the kernels are removed before cooking, the germ is lost and the nutritional value diminished.

Green peas. To retain maximum nourishment and flavour, always steam them in their pods, but wash them first. When the peas are adequately cooked, they can be easily podded. If the pods are young, they are often deliciously edible too, so nothing is wasted.

Zucchini. After light scrubbing, steam zucchini whole, taking care not to overcook. These are very tender vegetables, and they can easily be spoiled.

CARROT AND RAISIN SALAD

This is quite a departure from the style of main course salad offered thus far. The popularity of this taste combination as a side salad in leading restaurants, however, has been growing in recent years. This is not surprising, considering the increasing attraction to sweetness developing in the human palate. Indeed, this is a very sweet salad, but it is one that offers a vast array of possibilities. It can be served as a side salad by reducing the quantities suggested here, where it is given as a main course salad. No concentrated protein food should be eaten at the same meal as this salad if the most efficient digestion is desired. This is a high-energy salad, ideal for busy, active people.

NO COOKING REQUIRED — SERVES 4

INGREDIENTS

125 g natural seedless raisins
¾ cup pure apple juice
4 medium carrots
2 medium beetroot
2 stalks celery, chopped
⅓ cup chopped parsley
150 g fresh mushrooms, diced
1 red capsicum, cored and diced
½ cup fresh alfalfa sprouts
1 medium avocado

METHOD

1. Wash the raisins under running water; soak them in apple juice for at least an hour until they are plump; keep them covered to reduce oxidation.
2. Grate the carrots and beetroot and mix with the soaked raisins.
3. Add the celery, parsley, mushrooms, capsicum and sprouts to mixture and mix again.
4. Place the mixture in an attractive serving bowl and top with peeled and sliced avocado.

ALTERNATIVES

1. Sultanas can be used instead of raisins, but always use the "naturals", rather than those with the golden colour. Naturals are darker and have not been chemically treated during drying.
2. Fresh carrot juice can be used instead of apple juice, but it tends to not soak into raisins as well as apple juice does.
3. Mung bean or lentil sprouts can be used instead of alfalfa if desired. Alfalfa sprouts are the easiest to chew and digest.

TO SERVE

Any of the sweet breads in this book is an excellent accompaniment to this salad. This salad should not be left standing but should be eaten soon after completed preparation.

Fresh Salad Dressings

This is a group of luscious dressings designed to offer taste variety for people seeking more flavour from a salad than can be found in the ingredients alone. It is not usually possible to attain this from commercial dressings without introducing nutritional inhibitors. The dressings described here achieve this and provide nutritional advantages. The recipes are simple and contain only a few ingredients; their role in the salad is complementary rather than assertive.

TAHINI SALAD CREAM

Tahini (raw sesame butter) is an excellent salad dressing on its own, as is fresh lemon juice with which it is combined here. The addition of grated beetroot, ricotta cheese, and apple creates an amazingly delicious salad cream as well as enhancing nutrients and flavour. By slightly reducing the quantity of tahini, this cream can be made a little thicker and used as a pre-dinner dip, served with celery sticks and carrot strips.

NO COOKING REQUIRED BLENDING REQUIRED SERVES WITH A LARGE SALAD

INGREDIENTS
1 medium apple
3 tablespoons tahini
1 tablespoon fresh lemon juice
150 g fresh ricotta cheese, chopped
1 small beetroot, scrubbed and finely grated

METHOD
1 Core and dice the apple; leave the skin on.
2 Put tahini, lemon juice, ricotta, and apple in a blender.
3 Blend them until smooth, then add beetroot.
4 Continue to blend until the mixture is creamy.

ALTERNATIVES
1 To make a richer salad cream or pre-dinner dip, avocado can be added before the second blending.
2 Avocado can be a suitable replacement for cheese, but increase quantity of tahini to equal the amount of avocado.

TANGY AVOCADO DRESSING

The natural creaminess of the avocado lends a deliciously thick smoothness to this salad dressing. Combined with the tanginess of fresh lemon juice and the spicy flavour of fresh chives, it makes a most apealing salad dressing. All ingredients are nutritious: avocados especially for their generous quantities of essential fatty acids; lemon juice and chives for their vitamin C richness.

NO COOKING REQUIRED

SERVES WITH A LARGE SALAD

INGREDIENTS

2 medium avocados
1 tablespoon fresh lemon juice
1 tablespoon fresh chives, chopped

METHOD

1 Peel, stone and dice avocados.
2 Put all the ingredients into a shallow mixing bowl, and mash them until smooth.

ALTERNATIVES

1 If a more savoury flavour is preferred, replace lemon juice with 3 tablespoons of tahini.
2 This recipe converts to a delicious pre-dinner dip by adding another avocado: lemon juice or tahini or both can be used. Serve with celery and carrot sticks.

TO SERVE

Because avocado is classified as a fat-concentrate food, this dressing is better combined with a carbohydrate salad, such as potato or corn, than a protein-rich salad.

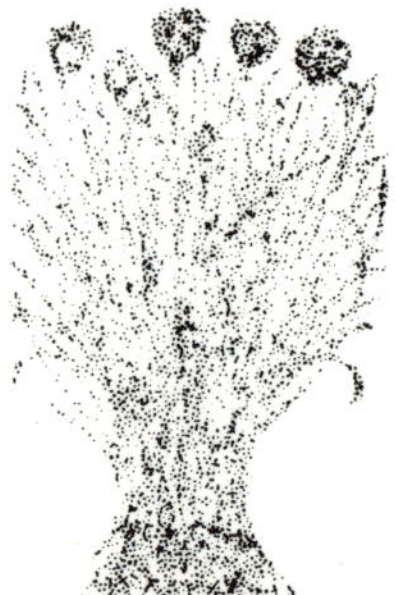

LOW-FAT SALAD CREAM

With a fat content of merely one-half of 1 per cent, this salad cream can be almost called "no-fat". It relies on uncreamed cottage cheese for its smoothness and is ideal for anyone who needs a fat-free diet to help counter obesity, hypertension, or cardiac problems.

NO COOKING REQUIRED BLENDING REQUIRED SERVES WITH A LARGE SALAD

INGREDIENTS
250 g uncreamed cottage cheese
2 slices ripe pineapple
2 tablespoons fresh lemon juice
1 teaspoon fresh mint leaves, chopped
a few sprigs of parsley

METHOD
1 Dice cheese and pineapple.
2 Put all the ingredients into a blender, lemon juice and pineapple first.
3 Blend at medium speed until smooth.

ALTERNATIVES
1 This is a tangy salad cream, but the taste can be made sweeter by substituting orange juice for lemon.
2 For a more savoury taste, tomato can be used instead of pineapple.

TO SERVE
This salad cream combines perfectly with a protein-rich vegetable salad, but it should not be used with a potato salad or any other salad in which starchy foods predominate.

INSTANT FRESH MAYONNAISE

Since it was developed over a century ago by the ingenious French as a flavour stimulant for cooked vegetables, mayonnaise has steadily become a universal favourite among salad dressings. But health-conscious diners tend to be cautious about its use, being alert to the possible dangers of salt, sugar, and hydrogenated chemically extracted oils. This recipe has been devised to satisfy those who also seek a little extra flavour and "creaminess" with their salad but want to avoid the contents of commercial mayonnaises. A further virtue of this mayonnaise is its comparative cheapness compared with the cost of top quality commercial mayonnaises.

NO COOKING REQUIRED BLENDING REQUIRED SERVES WITH A LARGE SALAD

INGREDIENTS

2 tablespoons fresh lemon juice
2 fresh egg yolks
½ teaspoon powdered vegetable seasoning (such as Dr Jensen's)
¾ cup cold-pressed vegetable oil

METHOD

1 Put the lemon juice, egg yolks and seasoning in blender.
2 Blend these slowly while adding the oil.
3 Pour into screw-top container and refrigerate.

ALTERNATIVES

The seasoning component lends itself to considerable creative variation. Alternatives such as mixed herbs, chopped mint, or a dash of apple cider vinegar can be tastefully used.

TO SERVE

This mayonnaise can be a successful complement with a cool vegetable salad or a plate of hot, steamed vegetables. It should always be stored in the refrigerator.

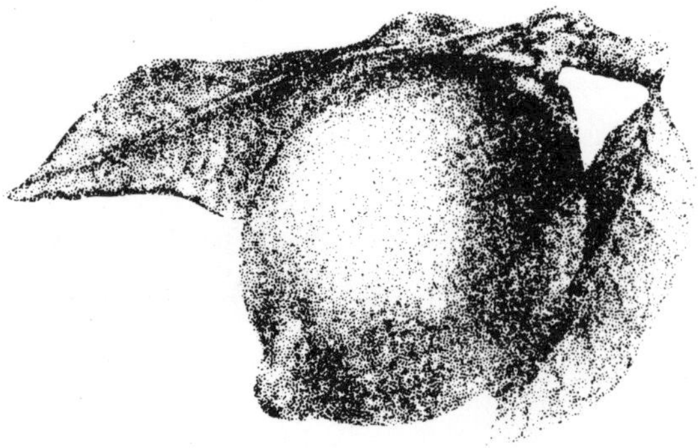

Group 3: Blender Delights

No kitchen appliance is more useful, for its size, than the blender. Many years of experience in devising menus and preparing nutritious meals have taught me that a blender is as important in my kitchen as a refrigerator. Sometimes I wonder how I ever managed without a blender — and to be sure I never have to again, I always keep a spare machine on hand, sometimes using both if preparing for special occasions. Of course, we can manage without almost anything, but the superb mixtures concoctable only with a blender tend to become an essential part of one's regular dietary habits.

All health-conscious cooks are familiar with at least some aspects of the versatility of a good blender. Indeed, many blender books are available, but they rarely rely on totally natural foods for their flavour, as is the intention of this book. The aim here is to provide a range of simple, yet creative, nutritional delights for a wide range of meals and occasions.

In a few other recipes throughout this book, I have specified the need for the blending of some ingredients. But in this special group of Blender Delights, all ingredients in every recipe are blended to attain the smooth consistency, without which the recipe would lack some of its special delectability. With the facility of the blender, these recipes convert the familiar flavours of a few individual ingredients into an appetising, velvet mixture with a flavour and texture providing a totally new dimension in taste.

Just as an artist, by careful and experienced mixing of individual colours, can generate a new shade of appealing beauty, so can the creative blending of flavoursome, natural foods give rise to deliciously different taste sensations. And this creativity can be very quickly developed.

Interesting and tasty variations to blender recipes can often result from a few slight alterations to ingredient proportions or by the alternative use of similar ingredients. I have suggested many such variations for most of these recipes, but the creative cook can soon develop many more with just a little experience in blender versatility.

Every ingredient in the following Blender Delights, as everywhere else in this book, is a wholesome and nutritious food. When such foods are combined so that their digestive properties are in balance, their blending will only confer improved nutritional advantages. The only nutrient losses that could occur from blending are the diminution of certain vitamins from exposure to air (oxidation). Vitamins B_1 and C are particularly sensitive, and folic acid and fat-soluble vitamins A and E are also sometimes affected. To avoid these losses, do not prepare blended foods in advance and store — prepare them just before mealtime.

Finally, a few words of advice with regard to the care of your precious blender. This machine can give well over a decade of faithful service, even when used daily. Never overload the blender motor. Always select a speed high enough to allow the motor sufficient power to perform its task comfortably. If the ingredients are hard substances (such as nuts), always use maximum speed. If ingredients are thick vegetables (such as coarse celery), selected three-quarters speed. For thick pieces of fruit (such as apple quarters), use half maximum speed. Always ensure fruit and vegetable blending is done with sufficient liquid by placing either the liquid ingredients or the softest and juiciest components in the blender jug first. If blending only liquids or very soft fruits, low speed will be adequate; the speed should be increased if a large quantity is to be blended. When a combination of different types of ingredients is to be blended, always choose the higher, rather than the lower, speed.

PAWPAW NECTAR

The versatility of the blender is here seen at its best in making a thick fruit nectar by combining the flesh from some of our most succulent fruits. When the heat of summer causes you to lose your appetite for a meal demanding lots of chewing, try this recipe for an exceptionally refreshing and nutritious "liquid meal". Or for those occasions when you seek a substantial between-meal drink, pawpaw nectar will become a favourite. Note how many tasty variations are possible, allowing for seasonal availability of fresh fruit and for the occasional demands of your taste buds.

NO COOKING REQUIRED BLENDING REQUIRED SERVES 6

INGREDIENTS

1 small pawpaw
3 cups pure apple juice
1 large banana, peeled
12 apricots, stoned
12 small ice cubes
½ tablespoon fresh mint leaves

METHOD

1 Remove the seeds from the pawpaw; scoop flesh into blender.
2 Pour the apple juice into the blender; add other ingredients.
3 Blend on medium speed until smooth (about a quarter of a minute).

ALTERNATIVES

1 Freshly squeezed orange juice can be used instead of apple juice (or use part of each) for a flavour variation.
2 Adding the juice of one lemon will give the nectar added tanginess.
3 Pure grape juice can also be used instead of apple juice (or use part of each) for increased sweetness.
4 Pure pear juice can be used instead of apple juice for further variety.
5 Fresh pineapple can be used instead of pawpaw (or use part of each).
6 Other fruits to try for variety include mango, mandarin, cantaloupe, peach, nectarine, and strawberry.

TO SERVE

Pour into glasses as soon as blended for immediate consumption to avoid any nutritional losses from oxidation. Do not drink it quickly: chew each mouthful for best digestion and maximum enjoyment of flavours. If the nectar is preferred colder, use more ice cubes in the mixture rather than refrigerating after blending. All the fruit, except the banana, can be refrigerated before blending to make a cooler mixture.

SPICY FRUIT PUNCH

This mixture of interesting flavours will provide a surprisingly refreshing and light drink for serving as a pre-dinner appetiser or a between meal pick-me-up. Based on boiled spearmint leaves (spearmint herb tea), this drink will refreshingly cleanse the palate and will be found to be most enjoyable on a hot day. As an evening drink to serve to guests at party-time or a social gathering, this fruit punch will be a winner, and it should be made in abundance. It is a welcome and nourishing departure from alcoholic beverages, which have destroyed more parties than they have made.

SOME HEATING REQUIRED   BLENDING REQUIRED   SERVES 6

INGREDIENTS

1 cup pure water
1 tablespoon dried chopped spearmint leaves (use as herb tea)
¾ teaspoon ground cinnamon
2 cups pure apple juice
1 cup pure grape juice
2 cups natural mineral water

METHOD

1 Boil pure water and pour it over the spearmint leaves in a cup.
2 Allow mixture to stand for a few minutes and stir to ensure thorough mixing.
3 Pour the mixture through a fine strainer and discard the spearmint leaves.
4 Add the cinnamon to the hot spearmint water and stir thoroughly.
5 Refrigerate until cold, then pour into blender.
6 Add apple and grape juices to blender and blend mixture on low speed for a few seconds until mixed.
7 Refrigerate in blender jug or other until needed.
8 Mineral water is added just before serving.

ALTERNATIVES

1 A little fresh lemon juice, or fresh orange juice, or both will provide a tangy variation in flavour if used instead of grape juice.
2 A natural cinnamon stick can be used instead of ground cinnamon by boiling it with the original cup of pure water before adding it to spearmint leaves.
3 Pear juice can be used instead of all or part of the apple or grape juice.

TO SERVE

Just before serving, pour the mixture into a suitable jug or punch bowl and add the mineral water. Stir well. Ice cubes can also be added. A few fresh mint leaves will also add colour and flavour when added before serving.

NIMBIN NUT CREAM

One of the most nutritious and simple meals is a basic fruit salad with raw, unsalted nuts. It is a protein-concentrated meal that also provides essential fatty acids, energy-giving carbohydrates, vitamins, and minerals. It is an easily digested meal suited to all needs, from the restful elderly to the athletic young — only the quantity needs to be varied. Many people, however, have problems with the inclusion of whole nuts in their meals and for various reasons avoid them. Whether one has dentures, diverticulitis, a hiatus hernia, or whatever, your blender will help you overcome the problem so that you are not deprived of these valuable protein sources. The simplicity and naturalness of this recipe symbolises its Aquarian Age origins, hence its name in honour of the northern New South Wales town of Nimbin, host of the Aquarius Festival of 1973, which gave the Age of Awareness its greatest single impetus in Australia.

NO COOKING REQUIRED BLENDING REQUIRED SERVES 2

INGREDIENTS

100 g raw unsalted almond kernels (naturals, not blanched)
3 medium oranges
1 large apple
100 g raw unsalted cashew nuts

METHOD

1 Remove the skins from the almonds by blanching them for 2 minutes in hot water, then rinsing in cold.
2 Peel and quarter oranges; put them in blender.
3 Scrub the skin of the apple, cut it into quarters, and remove the core; put in blender.
4 Add the nuts to the fruit and blend at maximum speed until smooth (half a minute).

ALTERNATIVES

1 For a variety of protein, vary the nuts at different meals by replacing almonds with brazils or hazelnuts; this also gives an interesting flavour variation. Other nuts are not so suitable for this recipe, but if your taste is flexible, try them.
2 A small apple and a small pear and be used instead of a large apple.
3 Two mandarins can be used instead of one of the oranges.
4 Many other fruits can be used to suit your taste needs, as long as sweet fruits are avoided. Try pawpaw, pineapple, deciduous summer fruits, a few seedless grapes or berries.

TO SERVE

1 Delicious on its own from a dessert bowl or parfait glass.
2 Can be served with a fresh fruit salad or a small vegetable salad.
3 Can be served as a dessert after a light salad or vegetable meal.
4 Many people enjoy this dish most after it has been cooled in the refrigerator.
5 Be sure to chew it thoroughly, even though it is a smooth cream, as this will ensure proper ensalivation and best digestion.

BLENDED NUT SALAD

Almost as simple as the blended nut-fruit salad (Nimbin Nut Cream), this blended nut and vegetable salad also provides an ideal way of overcoming any limitations in chewing and digesting such a salad in its whole state. And even if people have no denture problems and are not limited by a hiatus hernia or diverticulitis, there may be time limitations that would otherwise inhibit adequate chewing of nuts, celery, and capsicum, so the blending of these salad ingredients provides a valuable time and energy saving. So long as the recipe is prepared just prior to being eaten, almost no nutritional loss is incurred from oxidation or otherwise. Plus, the combining of these ingredients in the blender provides a flavour even more delightful than that from the sum of the individual components. This is a protein-rich meal which should be thoroughly chewed for best digestion.

NO COOKING REQUIRED BLENDING REQUIRED SERVES 2

INGREDIENTS

3 medium oranges
1 medium apple
1 medium capsicum, preferably red
100 g raw unsalted cashew nuts
100 g raw unsalted brazil nuts
2 stalks celery

METHOD

1 Peel and quarter oranges; put them in the blender.
2 Scrub the skin of the apple; cut the apple into quarters, remove the core; put the apple in the blender.
3 Scrub the capsicum; cut it into quarters; remove core; put capsicum pieces in blender.
4 Put the nuts in the blender.
5 Scrub the celery and trim any brown marks from the ends.
6 Start the blender directly to maximum speed; use the celery stalks to stir the mixture before allowing them to blend into mixture.
7 Blend until smooth; this could require up to one minute.

ALTERNATIVES

1 Nut variations can be used, as listed for Nimbin Nut Cream.
2 Cucumber and tomato can be included in the mixture, but most people prefer them cut on a plate and topped with the blended mixture.
3 Equivalent quantities of fresh pineapple can be used instead of one or two oranges.

TO SERVE

This blended salad can be poured into a large dessert plate and eaten as a cream. To increase the size and variety of ingredients, prepare a tomato and small cucumber by dicing them and placing in plate to be topped by the blended mixture. This can be further topped by alfalfa, lentil or mung bean sprouts. Ensure thorough chewing and enjoy these delicious flavours.

BLENDED RICOTTA FRUIT SALAD

Ricotta is a fresh cheese rapidly gaining popularity among health-conscious people, yet it was largely unheard of up to a few years ago. Italian in origin, ricotta cheese is prepared from whey and skim milk. As such, it is extremely low in fat (less than 2 per cent), yet high in protein (17 per cent). It contains a similar number of kilojoules to regular cottage cheese (4 per gram), which is less than half those found in an equivalent quantity of meat or bread. Ricotta is a smooth, white, uncured cheese with a short shelf life; it should be eaten within a day or two of being bought and kept no longer than a week. When mixed with the fruits in this recipe, a delicious, yet low kilojoule meal is the result.

NO COOKING REQUIRED BLENDING REQUIRED SERVES 2

INGREDIENTS

2 medium oranges
1 large apple
2 rings fresh pineapple
250 g fresh ricotta cheese
1 medium pawpaw

METHOD

1 Peel and quarter the oranges, then put them in the blender.
2 Scrub the skin of the apple; cut apple into quarters; remove core; put apple quarters in the blender.
3 Dice the pineapple after removing the core; put pieces in the blender.
4 Dice the ricotta and put in the blender.
5 Halve pawpaw lengthways; remove seeds.
6 Blend the mixture at medium speed until smooth (half a minute), then pour into pawpaw halves.

ALTERNATIVES

Any of the following fruits can be used instead of pawpaw, or in smaller quantities with pawpaw, as the base over which the ricotta cream is poured: pear, passionfruit, apricot, peach, nectarine, plum, cherry, strawberry, mulberry, blackberry, blueberry and kiwifruit.

TO SERVE

As the complete quantity of ricotta cream will not fit into each pawpaw half, pour the rest into a serving jug and put it on the table to be used as the meal is being consumed and more space is provided in each pawpaw half. This mixture should be prepared immediately before the meal, rather than in advance. If the cream is to be served cold, ensure that each component is cold before mixing.

Opposite: Spicy Fruit Punch (left) and Pawpaw Nectar (right) (see pages 33 and 32).

RICOTTA SALAD CREAM

This is the vegetable salad counterpart to the previous ricotta fruit salad. Instead of blending the entire salad, a creamy dressing is made in the blender from the ricotta cheese and some of the salad components, while the rest of the ricotta cheese is used in the salad. This replaces any need for a salad dressing. By using the ricotta cheese in both parts of the recipe, it also simplifies the demands on digestion by limiting the protein source to just one type. People suffering from ulcers will find this a most delicious and easily digested meal.

NO COOKING REQUIRED SOME BLENDING REQUIRED SERVES 2

INGREDIENTS

1 large orange
1 medium apple
250 g fresh ricotta cheese
2 stalks celery
1 medium tomato
1 small cucumber
1 medium capsicum, red preferred
½ cup mung bean sprouts
few sprigs parsley

METHOD

1 Peel and quarter the orange and put it in the blender.
2 Scrub the skin of the apple; cut the apple into quarters, remove core; put the quarters in the blender.
3 Dice the ricotta cheese and put a third of it into the blender.
4 Blend the mixture thoroughly on three-quarter speed, using one of the celery stalks to mix it before allowing it to blend into the ricotta cream.
5 Chop and dice the other celery stalk, the tomato, cucumber, and capsicum, and divide them between two plates together with the rest of the cheese.
6 Pour the ricotta cream equally over each salad plate.
7 Sprinkle mung beans and parsley on top of the ricotta cream.

ALTERNATIVES

1 Alfalfa or lentil sprouts can be used instead of mung beans.
2 Chopped fresh chives can be used in the blended mixture or sprinkled on top of each salad instead of parsley.
3 Any other fresh salad vegetable can be used instead of or as well as those suggested.
4 Swiss Emmenthaler cheese can be used instead of ricotta in the diced salad (but not in the blended salad cream).

TO SERVE

This is a complete meal, and it should be prepared just before serving to avoid oxidation of the vegetables and deterioration of the cheese.

Opposite top: Cashew Nut Loaf (see page 47).
Opposite bottom: Stuffed Mushrooms and Cauliflower Croquettes (see pages 57 and 51).

DAIRY-FREE MUESLI CEREAL

Muesli was originally developed at the Bircher-Benner Health Clinic in Zurich, Switzerland. The name "muesli" implies a whole grain cereal meal intended for consumption at breakfast-time. Over the decades since its development, muesli has been promoted throughout the health food industry, until now we find even the commercial breakfast cereal processors marketing a "muesli" as an "improvement" on their highly refined "lifeless" breakfast offerings. Some people prefer their muesli for lunch or for the evening meal, as it can be an excellent meal from which to derive sustained energy. But many modern mueslis are too complex, hence the offering of this recipe as a high-energy unrefined cereal combination making least demands on the body's digestive system. Nutrient-rich soya milk is used rather than animal milk, thereby avoiding allergy and respiratory-inhibiting risks of the latter.

NO COOKING REQUIRED BLENDING REQUIRED SERVES 1

INGREDIENTS: in blender
3 tablespoons instant soya milk powder
1 cup pure water
1–2 tablespoons pure maple syrup (vary to taste)

INGREDIENTS: in cereal bowl
2 tablespoons fresh raw wheat germ
1 tablespoon rice bran
1 tablespoon fresh rolled oats
1 tablespoon millet flakes

METHOD

1 Blend the ingredients in the blender at low speed until they are mixed (a quarter of a minute).
2 Pour the liquid over the cereal and stir in thoroughly to allow absorption.
3 Allow at least 15 minutes for the liquid to be absorbed into the cereal grains.

ALTERNATIVES

1 Added chewiness is provided by including natural raisins or sultanas in the cereal bowl; their added sweetness also allows for the reduction or elimination of maple syrup from the blended liquid.
2 Added B vitamins, protein, and minerals are provided when lecithin and nutritional yeast (up to 1 tablespoon of each) are added to the liquid.
3 Other rolled and flaked grains that can be used instead of or as well as oats and millet are wheat, corn, rye, and rice.
4 For added protein, soya flakes can be used instead of one of the cereals listed in the recipe.

TO SERVE

This muesli cereal is delicious served at room temperature, but if it is preferred cooled, put it in the refrigerator for stage 3 of Method; if it is preferred warm, put it over a saucepan of boiling water during stage 3 of the Method.

BLENDED BANANA CREAM

The banana is one of the most versatile of fruits, and it features in many recipes in this book. One of its special advantages is its ready availability during every month of the year. Nutritionally, it is a fruit with a well-balanced vitamin–mineral profile: it is especially rich in potassium and provides a ready source of fructose for quick energy. Take care when choosing bananas to avoid those that have been gas ripened; if necessary, buy green mature bananas and allow them to ripen naturally in a warm spot in your home. This allows the natural conversion of starch to sugar, resulting in optimum nutritional balance in the fruit, better keeping qualities, and better flavour.

NO COOKING REQUIRED   BLENDING REQUIRED   SERVES 2

INGREDIENTS

3 large ripe bananas, peeled and cut in halves
1 large apple, cored and quartered
100 g sun-dried dates, pitted

METHOD
1 Put bananas, apple, and dates into blender in that order.
2 Blend together until smooth at half full speed (about 1 minute).
3 Pour into serving containers or into parfait glasses.

ALTERNATIVES
1 Instead of a large apple, a small apple and a pear can be used.
2 Instead of all dates, 50 g each of dates and seeded raisins can be used.
3 If a little added spiciness is desired, add ½ teaspoon ground cinnamon.

TO SERVE
This recipe is very versatile. It can be used as a sweet cream for topping a fresh fruit salad (as long as acid fruits are not used, for they do not combine well with sweet fruits) or over any number of other suitable recipes in the final group in this book. It can also be served in parfait glasses as a sweet dessert, topped with a whole date or a pecan half kernel. Make this cream only just before serving, as it tends to oxidise quickly if not immediately eaten.

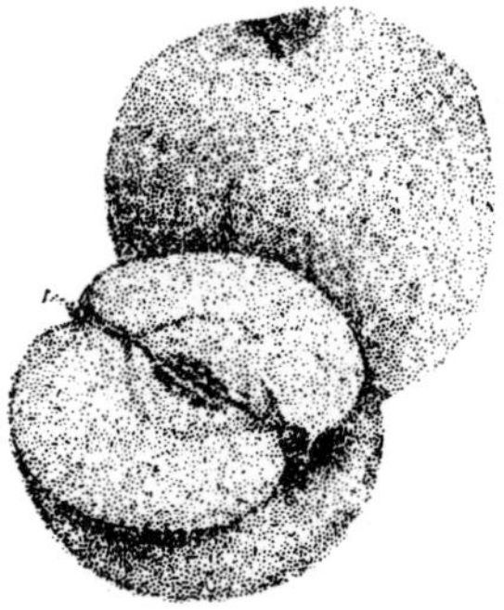

ATHLETE'S MILK SHAKE

One of the most universally enjoyed drinks is the milk shake. But in its usual composition of cow's milk, chemical-laden ice cream, and sugary flavouring, it represents digestive and dental horrors rather than nutritional benefits. By choosing wholesome ingredients, we can perform some nutritional alchemy. Based on non-allergic soya milk, this high-protein shake has the added benefits of providing high energy, vitamins, minerals, and even some essential dietary fibre and unsaturated fatty acids. For the busy, physically active person requiring a highly nutritious meal in a hurry, this mixture is an occasional boon, and it is also most delicious. This drink is extremely beneficial for the sportsperson after a heavy training session.

NO COOKING REQUIRED   BLENDING REQUIRED   SERVES 1

INGREDIENTS

2 large fresh yolks from open-range eggs
2 tablespoons instant soya milk powder
1 tablespoon fresh raw wheat germ
1 tablespoon lecithin powder or granules
½ tablespoon nutritional yeast (torula or brewer's)
2 tablespoons pure maple syrup
1 cup pure water

METHOD

1 Thoroughly separate egg yolks; discard the whites.
2 Blend all the ingredients together in a blender at three-quarters full speed.

ALTERNATIVES

1 For added protein, include a tablespoon of 95 per cent protein soy isolate powder.
2 Additional minerals are obtained by adding ½ teaspoon of kelp powder (this might necessitate an additional tablespoon maple syrup, depending on taste preferences).
3 A vitamin C and calcium boost is obtained by adding ½ teaspoon calcium ascorbate powder (equivalent to 2000 mg vitamin C).
4 Additional frothiness and coolness for the drink is obtained by adding a few ice cubes to the mixture before blending.

TO SERVE

Pour into large glass and drink slowly, "chewing" each mouthful to ensure adequate ensalivation. Remember, although this is a most delicious drink, it is also a very rich meal.

CAROB NIGHT CAP

Many people have acquired the habit of a hot drink before bed. Nutritionally, this is not suitable, unless one feels the need for some emotional calming (even then, meditation and soothing music are better). If a pre-bed drink is required, however, it should be nourishing and free from drugs, stimulants, refined sugar and the like. It is important to avoid chocolate, tea (unless valerian or chamomile herb tea), coffee, and acid-forming sweeteners. The following recipe avoids all these and uses only nutritious ingredients.

HEATING REQUIRED BLENDING REQUIRED SERVES 1

INGREDIENTS

1 teaspoon instant cereal beverage (such as coffee substitute)
1 teaspoon fine carob powder
2 teaspoons instant soya milk powder
1–2 teaspoons pure maple syrup (according to taste)
1 cup pure water

METHOD

1 Blend all the ingredients in a blender at low speed.
2 Pour the mixture into saucepan and gradually heat to drinking temperature, stirring to prevent sticking.

ALTERNATIVES

1 Goat's milk powder can be used instead of soya milk powder.
2 Honey can be used instead of maple syrup, although it is not as nutritious.
3 Instant dandelion "coffee" can be used as the cereal beverage.

TO SERVE

Pour the drink into a mug or cup for immediate consumption. In summer, this drink can be converted into a refreshing cool beverage by not heating it and just blending and cooling in refrigerator. Stir before pouring.

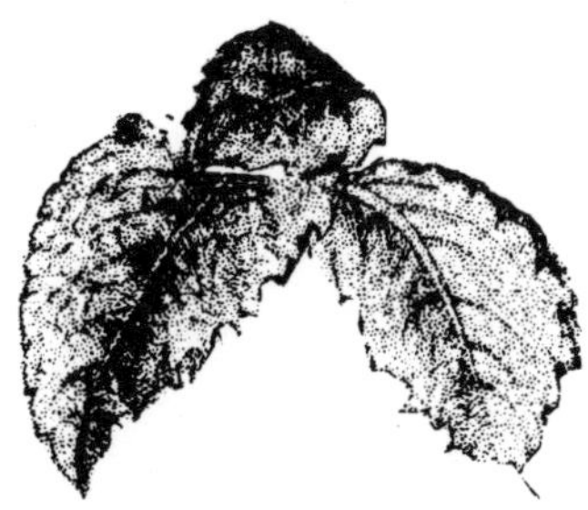

PART TWO

HEALTHFUL COOKING

Group 1: Protein-Rich Main Courses

As protein is the most essential nutrient in the human diet, care in its selection cannot be over-emphasised. Meat, fish, cheese, and eggs are featured in most recipes to further the promotion of their supporting industries. Yet those foods provide secondary proteins; they are less suited to man's digestive capacities than plant proteins. Furthermore, animal proteins are known sources of bacteria and undesirable chemicals, implying health risks that can be avoided.

Primary proteins are plant proteins. These are foods with concentrations of protein of more than 15 per cent by analysis. They include most nuts and seeds, such as almonds, cashews, brazils, hazelnuts, walnuts, pine nuts, pistachios, sunflower seed kernels, pepitas (pumpkin seed kernels), and sesame seeds. They are all rich in most minerals, especially calcium, as well as possessing all the amino acids essential for human needs.

All primary protein foods have a further valuable nutritional characteristic: their proteins are of simpler molecular structure than flesh proteins, so they are easier to assimilate. The digestive properties of nuts and seeds are, however, somewhat impaired when they are heavily roasted or salted; they should be eaten raw.

As most people eventually discover from painful experience, complex meals, in which foods abundant in protein, carbohydrates, and fats are mixed with sweet foods, will create digestion problems. This is avoided when protein-rich foods are eaten with raw vegetable salads or certain fruits (excluding bananas, dates, and other sweet fruits). And if healthful cooking habits are embraced, non-starch vegetables will also provide a suitable accompaniment to the digestion of protein.

Although not classified as primary protein foods, eggs and certain cheeses are easily digested by most people, and they are used frequently in the vegetarian diet of today. The matured and highly processed cheeses are to be avoided, for they are highly acid-forming in the body and high in sodium content, with its associated health risks and its inducement of an obsessive thirst. The most suitable cheeses are uncreamed cottage, ricotta, and Swiss Emmenthaler. Of the cheddar varieties, I only recommend Bodalla cheese, as it is the lowest in salt and the easiest to digest of local cheeses.

If eggs are to be used in the diet, the quantity consumed should be restricted, owing to their high level of cholesterol. This is, however, somewhat overcome by their natural lecithin. But lecithin is much lower in factory-farmed eggs than in eggs that are naturally produced and fertilised by free-range (or open-range) birds. Throughout this recipe book eggs are primarily used for their self-rising and mixture-binding properties, so their intake is kept low.

Cholesterol is a problem with all foods of animal origin eaten in large quantities. But it is not the only problem. Total absence of dietary fibre in animal foods, together with their lack of complex carbohydrates, has given rise to most of the modern health problems relating to the bowels. Animal meats, poultry, and seafood are, therefore, completely avoided in these recipes. Nuts and seeds are the primary protein recommendations, followed by soya beans and suitable cheeses. In fact, the last two are combined in a recipe for the making of soya cheese, which is totally free of animal products.

By carefully selecting the types of foods to be cooked and by ensuring that cooking is used just to soften the foods, nutritional loss is minimal, and the vegetables do not taste or look like an old soaked rag. For this reason, vegetables are preferably steamed, never boiled. If they are occasionally baked or casseroled for special dishes, this is never done at high temperatures and the period of cooking is minimal. The cooked dishes in this book are always heartily enjoyed, even by conventional meat-eating people — in fact they are amazed that a non-meat meal can taste so good, be so satisfying, and leave no after-thirst or uncomfortable fullness.

CASHEW NUT LOAF

There is probably no protein-rich food as sweet and delectable as cashew nuts. Originating in Brazil, the cashew nut is now grown on every continent except Australia, to where it is imported from India, Africa, China and Brazil. This recipe takes full advantage of the cashew's sweetness to mix with other protein-rich foods for baking into a savoury but sweet loaf. Especially when entertaining people used to eating meat, this recipe is an excellent substitute for the traditional meat loaf. Unlike meat, it is safe served hot or cold and, of course, is much more easily digestible.

PREHEAT OVEN TO 190° C (375° F) — SERVES 6

INGREDIENTS

2 large onions, peeled and diced
2 tablespoons cold-pressed vegetable oil
2 medium tomatoes, washed and diced
¼ teaspoon ground ginger
350 g raw unsalted cashew nut pieces
150 g mild cheddar cheese
½ cup fresh raw wheat germ
1 teaspoon mixed herbs
3 large open-range eggs

METHOD

1 Sauté onions in oil in a frypan until tender.
2 Add the tomatoes and ginger to frypan; cover, and simmer another 5 minutes.
3 Using a coffee grinder or similar, grind the cashew nuts into a coarse meal.
4 Grate the cheese into a large mixing bowl; add the cashews, wheat germ and herbs.
5 Mix the dry ingredients, then add the eggs and stir in.
6 Add the onion and tomato mixture to the large mixture and stir thoroughly.
7 Brush cold-pressed vegetable oil around the inside of a loaf dish to avoid sticking.
8 Pack the mixture into the loaf dish, eliminating any air pockets.
9 Bake until cooked through and light brown on top, usually 45 minutes.

ALTERNATIVES

1 If a more savoury flavour is wanted, use hazelnuts or brazils instead of some or all of the cashews. Do not use almonds, as they are too bland in flavour.
2 A further savoury flavour can be added in the form of chopped mushrooms. These should be added to the frypan when the tomatoes are added.

TO SERVE

Slice and serve hot with steamed zucchini, cauliflower or similar vegetables, or with a tossed salad. It can also be served cold with a salad, either sliced, or diced and tossed in the salad.

VEGETABLE AND NUT CUTLETS

The distinctive sweetness of cashew nuts is here combined with the more savoury brazil nut flavour to delight the creative culinary capers of even the most concerned cooks. And yet this recipe is so easy to prepare that even a novice bachelor cook will find it hard to foul up. The protein richness of these cutlets is supported by a large range of nutritious vegetables with a flavour guaranteed to become a favourite with many non-vegetarians, whether or not they seek to become converted to the vegetarian way.

PREHEAT OVEN TO 175° C (345° F) SERVES 6

INGREDIENTS

1 small eggplant, peeled and quartered
750 g butternut pumpkin, peeled, cut into large chunks and seeded
2 medium zucchinis, scrubbed and ends trimmed
500 g cauliflower
1 large onion, peeled and diced
1 tablespoon cold-pressed vegetable oil
1 teaspoon mixed herbs
¼ teaspoon ground ginger
2 large open-range eggs
250 g raw unsalted cashew nut pieces
250 g raw unsalted brazil nut pieces
150 g mild cheddar cheese
½ cup wheat germ

METHOD

1 Steam all the vegetables until tender.
2 Sauté the onion in oil in a frypan until it is light golden.
3 Mash all the steamed vegetables and mix in the onion, herbs and ginger.
4 Beat the eggs and mix into vegetables with the nuts and cheese.
5 Form mixture into desirable shapes — this is where creativity counts!
6 Roll each cutlet in wheat germ and place them on a well-oiled tray.
7 Bake the cutlets in the oven for 5 minutes at 175° C, then reduce to 150° C for a further 15–20 minutes, depending on size of cutlets (larger ones take longer to heat).

ALTERNATIVES

1 Nuts in these cutlets will be chewy; if this is not desired, grind the nuts into a coarse meal in coffee grinder or similar.
2 Almonds, walnuts, hazelnuts or pecans can be used instead of cashews or brazils, but be sure that all nuts are raw and unsalted.
3 If additional or varied seasoning is desired, Dr Jensen's Seasoning is suggested, as it is free from added common salt.
4 Sesame seeds can be used instead of wheat germ if desired.

TO SERVE

These are best eaten hot with steamed vegetables, such as peas or beans with broccoli, or with a freshly made salad.

SEVEN SEAS CASSEROLE

The simple vegetable casserole is probably the easiest cooked meal to prepare and it certainly requires no recipe. For added flavour dimensions, however, a little guidance will provide freedom from any nutritional inhibitors, such as salt, pepper, curry powder or other strong spices. For this recipe, the flavour variation converts a basic vegetable casserole to a protein-concentrate meal that can be complete in itself. Its name derives from the choice of ingredients: they are seven in number and each name begins with the letter "c". The name also implies the universality of this recipe.

PREHEAT OVEN TO 175° C (345° F) SERVES 6

INGREDIENTS

¼ medium green cabbage, coarsely shredded
¼ medium red cabbage, coarsely shredded
½ small cauliflower, broken into flowerets
2 medium carrots, thinly sliced
1 large capsicum, preferably red, cored and diced
2 medium chokos, halved and sliced (retain the core)
400 g mild cheddar cheese, grated

METHOD

1 Wash all the vegetables and place them in a large casserole dish and mix.
2 Cover the dish and place in the oven. Cook until just tender, about 30 minutes; this could be slightly longer if a deep dish is used.
3 Remove the cover and sprinkle grated cheese on top. Turn oven off.
4 Replace the cover and return the dish to the oven for 5 minutes for the cheese to melt into the vegetables, using the oven's stored heat.

ALTERNATIVES

1 To maintain the spirit of this recipe, chopped celery can be used instead of any suggested ingredient out of season.
2 Instead of cheddar cheese, cottage or ricotta cheese will provide a variation if they are cut into chunks and added just before serving; mix them into the vegetables and allow just two minutes in the oven.
3 For an added savoury flavour, add 1 teaspoon powdered vegetable seasoning before the casserole is first put in oven.
4 Any ground seeds or nuts can be used instead of cheeses at stage 3 of Method; the suggested quantity is at least 200 g, up to 300 g.

TO SERVE

This versatile dish can be served as a complete meal direct from the oven, as a part meal with a side salad, or as part of a buffet meal. Always serve hot.

CABBAGE AND CHEESE ROLLS

The idea for this recipe derives from the popular Greek dish dolmades. Instead of using grape vine leaves stuffed with rice, this recipe uses the more nutritious cabbage leaves with an even more nutritious stuffing, that of protein-rich soya beans with ricotta cheese. If possible, obtain a large red cabbage, for its nutritional and flavour properties are superior to any other type of cabbage — it is richer in protein, iron and vitamin C. Chinese cabbage is next in nutritional line, followed by savoy, and the usual white drumhead varieties.

PREHEAT OVEN TO 150° C (300° F) OVERNIGHT SOAKING REQUIRED SERVES 4

INGREDIENTS

250 g dry, raw soya beans
1 medium to large head cabbage
2 medium onions, peeled and chopped
2 tablespoons cold-pressed vegetable oil
1 red capsicum, cored and chopped
2 outer stalks celery (including leaves), chopped
1 tomato, finely chopped
¼ teaspoon ground ginger
100 g mushrooms, washed and diced
150 g fresh ricotta cheese
150 g mild cheddar cheese, grated

METHOD

1. Soak the soya beans in pure water overnight.
2. Next morning, rinse the soya beans and resoak until they are needed for cooking.
3. Steam the soya beans until tender, then mash them thoroughly.
4. Carefully remove 12 to 16 whole outer cabbage leaves from the head.
5. Steam the cabbage leaves until just tender.
6. Sauté the onions in oil until golden; then add capsicum, celery, tomato, ginger, and mushrooms and cook until just tender.
7. Thoroughly mix the sautéed vegetables, ricotta cheese, and soya beans.
8. Spread the cabbage leaves; cut out the centre stalk from each and place a large spoonful of mixture on the end nearest the centre stalk.
9. Carefully roll each cabbage leaf around the mixture, tucking in the sides.
10. Place cabbage rolls side by side on a shallow baking dish, top with grated cheese.
11. Place the rolls in the oven and turn temperature to off, as cheese will melt over rolls in stored heat. Allow 15 minutes for thorough heating.

ALTERNATIVES

1. If time does not permit using dry soya beans, use a 500 g can of "natural" soya beans, but drain off the liquid.
2. Garbanzos or lentils can be used instead of soya beans, but these are lower in protein.

TO SERVE

This can be a complete main course when served with a side salad or with steamed vegetables such as cauliflower and zucchinis. Always serve this meal hot and discard any left-overs, for reheated or cold cooked onions can often become digestive inhibitors.

CAULIFLOWER CROQUETTES

As a tasty and more nutritious variation of the standard favourite, cauliflower *au gratin*, this recipe is basically totally vegetarian, relying as it does on plant-source foods only. For those who want to use cheeses, variations with these are also offered. Either way, it makes for a most delicious dish, encouraging the use of the cook's creativity in shaping the croquettes to suit any special occasion, such as a birthday, graduation, wedding buffet or party. This imagination can provide great attractiveness for children, especially if they are "picky".

PREHEAT OVEN TO 175° C (345° F) SERVES 4

INGREDIENTS

1 medium or half a large cauliflower
1 medium eggplant, peeled and quartered
½ cup raw wheat germ
125 g raw tahini (sesame butter)
2 large open-range eggs, beaten thoroughly
3 tablespoons chopped fresh parsley
2 tablespoons chopped fresh chives
125 g raw hulled sesame seeds

METHOD

1 Steam the cauliflower and eggplant until tender.
2 Mash both thoroughly and add all other ingredients except sesame seeds.
3 The mixture should be stiff and suitable for shaping; if not, add more wheat germ.
4 Create suitable shapes for croquettes; cover all over with sesame seeds.
5 Place the croquettes on a flat baking tray in the oven until heated through, usually 20 minutes.

ALTERNATIVES

1 Instead of wheat germ, bran or half of each can be used.
2 Instead of tahini, raw cashew butter can be used, but this will give a sweeter overall taste; tahini is more savoury.
3 Instead of sesame seeds, grated cheddar cheese can be used, in which case it only needs to be sprinkled on top just before removing croquettes from oven.
4 Instead of making this mixture into croquette shapes and dipping in sesame seeds, it can be packed into an oiled loaf tin, topped with sesame seeds (or cheese), and baked for half an hour. For this variation, add an extra egg to the mixture.

TO SERVE

This meal must be served hot, and it is ideal accompanied by a tossed salad. Alternatively, it can be served with steamed green vegetables, such as asparagus (not canned), brussels sprouts and/or green beans. Steamed carrots also combine nicely with this meal.

PROTEIN–CAROTENE LOAF

Vitamin A nourishes eyes, skin, bones, and teeth. And many people want to know how they can get more vitamin A (carotene) into their diets when they eat cooked food. Fortunately, moderate cooking does not destroy vitamin A (as it does vitamins B_1 and C), so many carotene-rich foods can be combined in one nourishing recipe in which protein is also a nutritional feature. The two major protein sources chosen (eggs and cheddar cheese) are the only protein-rich foods that contain reasonable quantities of vitamin A — nuts and seeds rarely offer more than traces of vitamin A, with the exception of pistachio nuts, which are here offered as a supplement to cheese.

PREHEAT OVEN TO 175° C (345° F) SERVES 6

INGREDIENTS

10 leaves silverbeet
500 g carrots, scrubbed and trimmed
4 large open-range eggs, beaten
150 g raw pistachio nut kernels
200 g mild cheddar cheese
3 tablespoons chopped fresh parsley
100 g mushrooms, washed and chopped
1 teaspoon mixed herbs
1 teaspoon salt-free vegetable seasoning (e.g. Dr Jensen's)

METHOD

1 Trim the white centre stalks from the silverbeet and steam leaves until tender, then chop thoroughly.
2 Finely grate the carrots and mix with the eggs.
3 Using a coffee grinder or similar, grind nuts into a coarse meal.
4 Grate the cheese into a large mixing bowl and mix in all the other ingredients.
5 Brush cold-pressed vegetable oil around the inside of a loaf dish to avoid sticking.
6 Pack the mixture into the loaf dish; eliminate any air pockets.
7 Bake until cooked through and light brown on top — usually 45 minutes.

ALTERNATIVES

1 A sprinkling of sesame seed kernels on top can be added before baking.
2 If additional savouriness is desired, a large onion, sautéed in cold-pressed vegetable oil, can be used; this recipe, however, is very flavoursome as it is.

TO SERVE

Slice the loaf and serve it hot with steamed cauliflower, broccoli, green peas or similar vegetables. It is also delicious served with a large salad. This loaf can be successfully served cold with either a salad or steamed vegetables; serve it sliced or diced and tossed into salad. This loaf is also delicious topped with Aubergine Sauce (page 60).

Opposite: Savoury Lentil Surprise (see page 65).

COTTAGE CHEESE BAKE

Traditions are a vital part of our culture. And many traditions relating to food are not easily broken (although they can certainly be bent). The meat loaf is just one of these traditions that vegetarians can bend, as illustrated by the two preceding recipes. This recipe is a further example of a high-protein baked loaf that not only has more flavour than its traditional forerunner, but is also more easily digested, healthier, and it can be eaten next day cold without fear of salmonella developing. Additional protein concentration is provided here by the eggs, wheat germ, soya milk powder, and sesame seeds.

PREHEAT OVEN TO 175° C (345° F) SERVES 6

INGREDIENTS

4 medium zucchinis, washed and trimmed
500 g fresh cottage cheese
3 large open-range eggs, beaten
1 cup raw wheat germ
2 tablespoons instant soya milk powder
100 g mushrooms, washed and chopped
3 tablespoons chopped fresh chives
4 tablespoons raw tahini (sesame butter)
2 tablespoons hulled sesame seeds

METHOD

1 Steam the zucchinis until they are just tender; chop into small pieces.
2 Mash the cottage cheese until smooth, then mix it with the eggs.
3 Mix all the ingredients, except sesame seeds, thoroughly in a large bowl.
4 Pack the mixture into a well-oiled loaf dish, eliminating any air pockets.
5 Sprinkle sesame seeds on top, pushing them into mixture with back of spoon.
6 Bake until cooked through — about 1 hour.

ALTERNATIVES

1 Instead of zucchinis, eggplant can be used for a tasty variation.
2 Another alternative to zucchinis is the pulp of juiced carrots: if this is used, an additional egg is recommended or a reduction of wheat germ to ½ or ¾ cup.
3 A different result from this recipe can be obtained by baking the mixture in a shallow dish for about 45 minutes. In this case, 3 tablespoons sesame seeds will be required, or grated cheddar cheese can be used, as a topping.

TO SERVE

When made as a loaf, serve it sliced; as a shallow bake, serve it by spoon. This recipe is delicious served either hot or cold (although cheese topping should not be used if it is intended for cold serving). It can be accompanied by steamed vegetables, such as brussels sprouts and cauliflower, or by a large tossed salad.

Opposite: Capsicum Caprice (see page 67).

HIGH-PROTEIN CUSTARD

We usually regard baked custard as a dessert to follow the main course of a meal, but this is not necessarily so. For centuries, the custard has been a favourite cooked liquid mixture of milk, eggs and sweetening, but the nutritional qualities of those three ingredients have deteriorated so much since the Industrial Revolution that today's usual custard is anything but healthy. In this recipe, animal milk is avoided, sweetening is not artificial or refined, and the skilful addition of other protein-rich ingredients contribute to make such a wholesome custard that it provides a most satisfying meal in itself, with especially high protein qualities.

PREHEAT OVEN TO 150° C (300° F) BLENDING REQUIRED SERVES 6

INGREDIENTS

2 tablespoons instant soya milk powder
2 tablespoons high-protein powder (use only isolated soya protein powder)
5 cups pure water
4 large fresh open-range eggs
100 g finely ground cashew nut meal
2 tablespoons lecithin powder or granules
1 level tablespoon nutritional yeast (torula or brewer's)
3 tablespoons pure maple syrup

METHOD

1. Blend all the ingredients together in blender at three-quarters full speed. It is generally necessary to blend in two stages, using half the ingredients at a time.
2. Pour the mixture into a large, deep casserole dish.
3. Stand the casserole dish in a larger flatter ovenware dish that has been half-filled with hot water.
4. Place dishes in oven; do not cover.
5. After baking for 15 minutes, reduce the oven temperature to 120° C (250° F).
6. Bake until just set — about 1½ hours total time.

ALTERNATIVES

1. Finely ground almond meal can be used instead of cashew meal, but it is not quite as sweet, so the maple syrup should be increased to 4 tablespoons.
2. A sprinkling of nutmeg or cinnamon on top can be used if desired.

TO SERVE

As this is a concentrated protein meal, it can be served with non-sweet fruit (such as apricots, peaches, pawpaw) or, even better, eaten on its own as the total meal. It is an ideal lunch or light evening meal; some people enjoy it for breakfast if they have been up for a while and undergone an energetic exercise programme. It is best served from the refrigerator.

BEAN SPROUT OMELETTE

The Americanised version of Chinese cooking has become so popular throughout Australia since the Second World War that it is now considered a part of the traditional Australian eating-out habit. We call it Chinese food, but many of the dishes to be found in a Chinese restaurant in the West bear little relationship to authentic Chinese food. One dish that does, however, is the bean sprout omelette, for this is so flavoursome that it does not need the pernicious additives of monosodium glutamate, common salt, or other digestive inhibitors. This recipe is based on the Chinese idea of bean sprout omelette, for the mung bean has become accepted as typical of Chinese cooking; the use here of ricotta cheese lends more of an Italian variation while providing increased protein availability.

COOK IN SHALLOW COVERED FRYPAN SERVES 2

INGREDIENTS

1 large onion, peeled and chopped
2 tablespoons cold-pressed vegetable oil
1 medium capsicum, cored and chopped
1 stalk celery, chopped
¼ teaspoon ground ginger
6 large open-range eggs
200 g fresh ricotta cheese
½ cup fresh sprouted mung beans
50 g mild cheddar cheese, grated

METHOD
1 Sauté the onion in oil until it is golden.
2 Add the capsicum, celery, and ginger; stir and sauté for a further 5 minutes.
3 Thoroughly beat the eggs; dice the ricotta cheese; mix them together.
4 Add the eggs and ricotta to the sautéed mixture in frypan, cover and allow to cook over moderate heat for 5 minutes until egg begins to harden on the bottom.
5 With a large spatula, turn the mixture over, and sprinkle the sprouts on top.
6 Cover for a further 5 minutes, then sprinkle cheddar cheese over the sprouts.
7 Again cover and turn off the heat; allow the omelette to stand for a further 5 minutes.

ALTERNATIVES
1 A variety of vegetables can be used instead of or as well as celery and capsicum, such as mushrooms (diced), tomato (chopped) and eggplant (peeled, pre-steamed and mashed).
2 Instead of mung bean sprouts, sprouted lentils can be used.

TO SERVE
Serve hot as soon as it is ready, accompanied by a tossed salad or steamed vegetables, such as broccoli and carrots.

EGGPLANT PARMESAN

Parmesan cheese takes its name from the Italian town famous for its processing. It is a hard, rather dry cheese, favoured by chefs whenever grated cheese is required. However, it is a very salty cheese and for this reason is avoided by nutritionally conscious chefs. Its most suitable replacement among local cheeses is any low-salt block cheese (for example, the mild Bodalla or Norco cheeses of New South Wales). Another nutritionally motivated substitution, by which traditional eggplant parmesan is converted to a more nutritious meal, is the use of raw wheat germ instead of white flour. This is a somewhat radical departure from the European concept of eggplant parmesan, but it does result in a far healthier version of the *cordon bleu* favourite.

COOK IN OPEN FRYPAN; PREHEAT OVEN TO 150° C (300° F) SERVES 4

INGREDIENTS

8 small zucchinis
2 medium eggplants
½ cup cold-pressed vegetable oil
2 large open-range eggs, beaten
1 cup raw wheat germ
3 medium tomatoes, sliced thinly
100 g small mushrooms, sliced
400 g mild cheddar cheese, grated

METHOD

1 Lightly steam the zucchinis for 5 to 10 minutes, until just tender.
2 Slice the eggplants about 6 mm thick.
3 Pour the oil into a frypan and heat to just below boiling point.
4 Dip the slices of eggplant into egg until covered, then into wheat germ until covered, then put in the frypan and cook until just tender on first side (about 3 to 4 minutes), then turn over for same period until just tender.
5 As the eggplant becomes cooked, remove, and place on few thicknesses of kitchen paper towels to absorb the excess oil.
6 Into a suitable casserole dish, place layers of eggplant, tomato, sliced zucchini and mushrooms, then sprinkle with grated cheddar cheese.
7 Repeat these layers until all the ingredients are used, sprinkling cheese over each layer and on top.
8 Cover the casserole and put it in the oven for 15 minutes, until heated through.

ALTERNATIVES

1 Instead of wheat germ, bran or a coarse wholemeal can be used.
2 Added seasoning can be obtained from a light sprinkling of powdered salt-free vegetable seasoning (such as Dr Jensen's) over the tomato layers.

TO SERVE

As with most protein-rich hot meals, this is best combined with a fresh vegetable salad or steamed vegetables such as cauliflower and carrots.

STUFFED MUSHROOMS

A delicious combination of three nutritious foods, topped with grated cheese, makes this recipe one of my favourites when entertaining. Be sure to choose large mushrooms that are fresh and unbruised, for they must be kept whole. Mushrooms are among the most nutritious of vegetables (but take care, as some people are allergic to them), being one of the richest vegetarian sources of niacin. For weight-conscious people, it is good to know that mushrooms are low in kilojoules (less than 1 per gram weight) and yet have 2.2 per cent protein. Two other nutritious foods in this recipe are avocado and tahini (sesame butter, made from the grinding of hulled sesame seeds). When combined with the cheese, this recipe is justifiably classified as protein-rich.

COOK IN LARGE COVERED FRYPAN | SERVES 4

INGREDIENTS

8 large whole mushrooms
2 tablespoons cold-pressed vegetable oil
1 large (or 2 small) avocado
6 tablespoons tahini
200 g mild cheddar cheese, grated

METHOD

1. Carefully wash the mushrooms and remove stalks.
2. Heat the oil in the frypan to moderate.
3. Place the mushrooms in the frypan with stalk ends up, cover, and simmer at a slightly reduced temperature for 5 minutes.
4. Meanwhile, mash the avocado flesh and tahini into a smooth paste.
5. With a spatula, carefully remove the mushrooms from the frypan and place on a large plate; pack the avocado-tahini mixture into the mushrooms and top them with grated cheese.
6. Return the stuffed mushrooms to frypan, cover, and simmer at a low temperature for 5 minutes until the cheese melts and the mixture is heated through.

ALTERNATIVES

1. Olives or capers (sliced) can be used to top mushrooms instead of (or as well as) cheese.
2. A sprinkling of hulled sesame seeds can be used instead of cheese; in this case, the final simmering will need to be for 10 minutes.

TO SERVE

These are ideal served with Seven Seas Casserole (page 49) or Cauliflower Croquettes (page 51); they also combine perfectly with a fresh salad.

MEATLESS BOLOGNESE SAUCE

There is no reason for vegetarians to be deprived of an occasional spaghetti bolognese just because the traditional bolognese sauce is meat-based. Vegetarian inventiveness has created a far healthier and even tastier equivalent. It is a non-cholesterol, soya-bean-based companion to wholemeal spaghetti or it can be used as a topping on a protein-rich main course. (If choosing spaghetti or other pasta, favour wholemeal varieties, rather than the usual varieties which are made from white refined flour. Buckwheat pasta is also more nourishing than wheat varieties, although it is often more difficult to obtain.)

COOK IN FRYPAN ON MEDIUM TEMPERATURE — SERVES 4 TO 6

INGREDIENTS

1 cup pure water
100 g TVP "Beef-style" mince
2 medium onions, peeled and chopped
2 tablespoons cold-pressed vegetable oil
2 large tomatoes, chopped
100 g mushrooms, chopped
1 teaspoon mixed herbs
¼ teaspoon ground ginger

METHOD

1 Bring the water to the boil; add the TVP; remove from heat and allow to stand 30 minutes.
2 Put the expanded TVP in colander and rinse it under hot running water, then drain for at least 5 minutes.
3 While the TVP is soaking, sauté the onions in the oil until tender, then add the tomatoes, mushrooms, herbs, and ginger.
4 Cover the frypan and simmer for 10 to 15 minutes, stirring occasionally.
5 Add the TVP to the frypan mixture; mix thoroughly; replace the lid and simmer on a low temperature for a further 10 minutes until it is thoroughly heated.

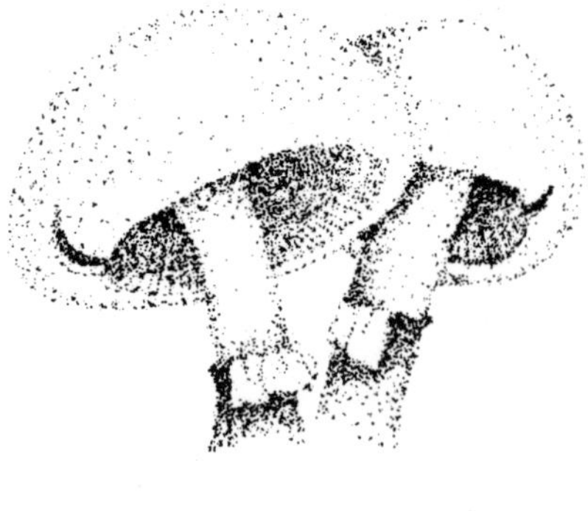

What Is TVP?

When meat prices in supermarkets skyrocketed and cholesterol jumped to unsafe levels in human bloodstreams, many manufacturing concerns turned their developmental resources to providing a meat substitute that offered a high level of food protein without the disadvantages of animal meats. The A.D.M. Company of Decatur, Illinois, was most successful in their development of TVP.

TVP is the trade name, registered by A.D.M., for Textured Vegetable Protein, which they have successfully produced from soya beans. It is prepared from nature's highest protein food, and retains most of the nutrients possessed by soya beans. Numerous flavourings and seasonings have been added so that the end product resembles different animal meats in all but appearance and fattiness.

Vegetable and herb derivatives are used to flavour TVP, as is common salt. This last ingredient is the most unsatisfactory, as far as human nutrition is concerned. As salt is so soluble, much of it can be removed from TVP by rinsing it thoroughly in warm water after a half hour of soaking. But on the plus side, TVP is designed to attract habitual meat eaters away from their high-cholesterol addiction by offering a non-cholesterol alternative with a very high protein content.

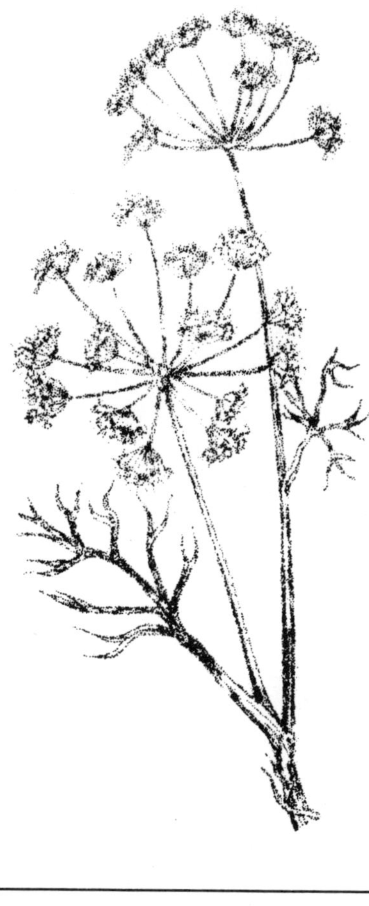

AUBERGINE SAUCE

There are no special nutritional properties in eggplant, but it is a tasty and alkalising vegetable with a wide versatility that lends it to frequent use by discriminating chefs. In this recipe, the smooth tenderness of steamed eggplant is combined with equally versatile tahini and tomato to provide a delicious sauce for use over almost any cooked meal, especially a protein-rich recipe, for which flour-based sauces or gravies are unsuitable.

STEAMING REQUIRED SERVES 4

INGREDIENTS
1 medium eggplant
6 tablespoons tahini
1 medium tomato, finely chopped
50 g mushrooms, washed and finely chopped
1 teaspoon salt-free powdered vegetable seasoning (e.g. Dr Jensen's)

METHOD
1 Steam the eggplant until very soft, then peel and mash it thoroughly.
2 Mix the tahini with the eggplant; add the tomato, mushrooms and seasoning.
3 Thoroughly mash the mixture; pour it into a saucepan; cover and simmer at a low temperature until it is heated through.

ALTERNATIVES
1 Instead of powdered seasoning, use mixed herbs.
2 Sautéed onion can be used as an additional seasoning.

TO SERVE
This sauce can be served over any steamed vegetables or over any other cooked recipe in this book. It should be served hot and will nutritionally combine with almost any type of meal.

Group 2: Fibre-Rich Main Courses

Now that the Western world has at last been awakened to the dietary problems caused by a deficiency of fibre in processed foods, emphasis in nutrition is being directed toward providing adequate bran or other high-fibre "roughage" in the diet. This is necessary to compensate for the refining and fragmenting of whole foods by modern industrial processes. It is at best a partial compensation, an apology to nature, so to speak, that does not go far enough.

Most nutritionists now agree that bran is an excellent dietary supplement. Yet few are prepared to suggest that, instead of supplementing an inadequate diet, people should remove from their diet the components that are deficient in so many essential nutrients. Such deficiencies should be made good by nutrient-rich whole foods, especially those with adequate dietary fibre content.

Buckwheat is just such a food. It is one of nature's richest sources of dietary fibre, and it offers more general nutritional benefits than any other grain. My number one choice of grain is, therefore, buckwheat.

Wherever possible in this book, buckwheat is chosen in preference to wheat or any other grain. Far too much reliance is placed on wheat in the modern diet, yet it is only fourth on the list of grains in terms of nutritional richness. After buckwheat come millet and oats. After wheat, come rye, rice, barley, and corn. The nutritional properties for which wheat generally finds favour are B-vitamins, protein, and fibre, yet in none of these does it excel. Its general fibre content is less than a quarter that of buckwheat (and once the bran is removed in refining, the fibre residue is barely registrable), and its protein is nutritionally unbalanced. Wheat is significantly low in the essential amino acid lysine, as is rye, and both are high in gluten, which is a problem for people (especially children) suffering from coeliac disease. For this reason, no grains should be fed to infants before the age of eighteen months, and then only sparingly until they have most of their first teeth.

Because the modern diet places so much emphasis on processed foodstuffs, most grains come to us robbed of their roughage (fibre) and nutritional core (the "germ"). This is especially evident in the milling of wheat and rice throughout the world. For this reason, only whole grains are ever recommended in this book; even the "enriched" flours are avoided, for these are nothing but admissions that too many nutrients were robbed in the milling process.

This is the reason why in this recipe book, I suggest meals based on the use of whole foods, free of refined grains, digestive inhibitors, and nutritionally harmful substances. In particular, the following group of recipes has been selected for its emphasis on at least one primary ingredient rich in natural dietary fibre and all ingredients have proven nutritional benefits and appetising deliciousness.

KASHA NATURA

It is appropriate that the first fibre-rich recipe should feature buckwheat, for no whole food offers more dietary fibre. And, unlike wheat bran, it has a most enjoyable flavour which is, of course, one of the factors in its long history of use, dating from pre-scientific times when foods were only chosen for their taste and ease of availability. Buckwheat amply satisfies both criteria, for it is a hardy cereal crop that can adapt to harsh climates without sacrificing its nutritional properties. It has been a staple food of the rugged Russian peasants for countless centuries; they took it westwards to Europe, to America and, more recently, Australia. The buckwheat cereal preparation known as "kasha" is as much the favourite of Russians as is rice for the Orientals and corn for the Mexicans. But buckwheat is by far the most nutritious. To capitalise on its healthful properties, buckwheat is here prepared in the most natural manner. This basic recipe provides the essence for a delicious breakfast cereal, as well as for a host of savoury dinner ideas, some of which follow.

COOK IN DOUBLE BOILER — A BASIC RECIPE

INGREDIENTS

2¾ cups pure water
250 g raw whole buckwheat kernels (1⅓ cups)

METHOD

1. Bring pure water to the boil in a saucepan or kettle.
2. Meanwhile, boil a cup of tap water in the bottom of a double boiler.
3. Pour the boiling pure water into the top of the double boiler and add the buckwheat.
4. Immediately cover the saucepan, reduce heat to low, and simmer for about 30 minutes until tender and all the pure water is absorbed. Do not stir.
5. Turn off the heat and allow the buckwheat to stand unmoved and still covered for a further 20 to 30 minutes.
6. Carefully remove the saucepan lid, ensuring that condensation does not run onto the buckwheat. Allow the buckwheat to stand another 5 minutes.

TO SERVE

The buckwheat is now fully cooked and quite "fluffy", with a light looseness that enables it to be used for a wide variety of dishes. Buckwheat can be either used immediately it is cooked or can be stored after cooling. When storing, be sure to allow it to remain light and loose by not packing it tightly into a storage container. Use a spacious, covered container for overnight storage in a refrigerator.

BUCKWHEAT BREAKFAST MUESLI

As a most nutritious and delicious development of the previous Dairy-Free Muesli Cereal breakfast (see recipe on page 38), buckwheat and other fibre-rich ingredients are gathered here to provide an ideal start-of-day meal. For many people with a history of bowel sluggishness or chronic bowel problems, this can be a most beneficial breakfast. Its high nutritional level also provides substantial B-vitamins, protein, and alkalising minerals, making this a rather powerful meal, whether it be served for breakfast, lunch, or for the evening meal.

NO COOKING REQUIRED (once buckwheat is prepared) BLENDING REQUIRED SERVES 1

INGREDIENTS: in blender

3 tablespoons instant soya milk powder
½ tablespoon pure carob powder
½ tablespoon pure lecithin granules (or powder)
1 tablespoon pure maple syrup
1 cup pure water

INGREDIENTS: in cereal bowl

3 tablespoons Kasha Natura (recipe page 62)
1 tablespoon rice bran
1 tablespoon fresh raw wheat germ
1 tablespoon pure desiccated coconut

METHOD

1 Blend the ingredients in the blender at low speed until mixed (a quarter of a minute).
2 Pour the liquid over the cereal and stir thoroughly to allow absorption.
3 Allow at least 15 minutes for the liquid to be absorbed into the cereal.

ALTERNATIVES

For added sweetness and dietary fibre, diced sun-dried pears and or figs can be included, but only in small quantities to avoid the risk of indigestion from an overload of sweetness in the stomach while the protein of the cereal is being digested.

TO SERVE

This meal is quite versatile, and it can be served warmed in winter, at room temperature in mid-season, or cool from the refrigerator on a hot summer day. If desired warm, place it on top of a saucepan of boiling water during stage 3 of the Method.

SAVOURY KASHA CASSEROLE

By using the vast array of flavours and textures made available to us from the vegetable kingdom, and by the judicious application of a few herbs, the simple flavour of the basic Kasha Natura recipe can be converted into a savoury casserole to delight the most discriminating palate. This then becomes a main course meal with a variety of serving ideas. It is easy to prepare and to digest; it is especially enjoyable on a cool winter's night.

PREHEAT OVEN TO 150° C (300° F) SERVES 4
Utensils needed: double boiler, covered frypan, covered casserole dish

INGREDIENTS
2 medium onions, peeled and chopped
2 tablespoons cold-pressed vegetable oil
1 large red capsicum, cored and diced
2 stalks celery (including leaves), chopped
4 small zucchinis, thinly sliced
100 g fresh mushrooms, sliced
¼ teaspoon ground ginger
½ cup mung bean sprouts
½ teaspoon mixed herbs
1 complete recipe Kasha Natura (page 62)

METHOD
1 Sauté the onions in the oil until light golden.
2 Add the capsicum, celery, zucchinis, mushrooms and ginger to the onions; cover and cook until tender (about 10 minutes).
3 Place the empty casserole dish in the oven to pre-warm.
4 Add the sprouts and herbs to the frypan, mix and heat through for a further 2 to 3 minutes.
5 Empty the buckwheat from the double boiler into the casserole dish and mix all the other ingredients thoroughly with it.
6 Cover the casserole dish; put it in the oven; turn the oven off (to conserve electricity or gas). Allow 10 to 15 minutes to heat through before serving.

ALTERNATIVES
1 Instead of sautéed onions, a savoury flavour can be obtained by using tahini; steam the vegetables and mix them thoroughly in tahini before combining them with the buckwheat.
2 Instead of mixed herbs, the same quantity of powdered vegetable seasoning (e.g. Dr Jensen's) can be used, as long as it is salt-free.
3 Fresh lentil sprouts can be used instead of mung bean sprouts.

TO SERVE
This casserole can be served as a most satisfying complete meal. It can also be accompanied by a tossed salad or by additional steamed vegetables, such as cauliflower and carrots, potato or pumpkin.

SAVOURY LENTIL SURPRISE

Few people realise the superb flavours to be derived from the judicious combining of certain cooked vegetables. And when these flavours derive from such nutritional sources as lentils or garbanzos, mushrooms, olives, chives, carrots, and capsicums, we indeed have a bonanza to serve with pride and pleasure as a valuable component of any meal. Both lentils and garbanzos (chickpeas) are fibre-rich, and they offer substantial protein, complex carbohydrates, iron, and potassium; they are also low in fats. Using either of these delicious legumes, this basic recipe becomes a satisfying meal on its own, or it can be incorporated with other ingredients, as in some of the following recipes in this group and in the sandwich section.

PRESOAK LENTILS — PREHEAT OVEN TO 150° C (300° F) — SERVES 4
Utensils needed: steaming saucepan, large covered frypan, covered casserole dish

INGREDIENTS

250 g dry brown lentils (or garbanzos)
2 cups pure water
100 g whole black olives, drained
2 tablespoons cold-pressed vegetable oil
150 g fresh mushrooms, sliced
1 large green capsicum, cored and diced
¼ teaspoon ground ginger
3 medium carrots, scrubbed
2 tablespoons fresh chives, chopped
1 teaspoon mixed herbs

METHOD

1 Soak the lentils in water for at least 8 hours before cooking.
2 Rinse the lentils under tap water when soaked, then steam them until tender (about 30 minutes).
3 Meanwhile, finely chop the olives after removing seeds.
4 Place 1 tablespoon oil in the frypan and bring it to medium heat.
5 Add the mushrooms, capsicum, and ginger to the frypan; cover and cook for 5 minutes.
6 Meanwhile, grate carrots, sprinkle them with the rest of the oil and toss thoroughly (to minimise oxidation).
7 Add the grated carrot to the frypan; mix it in; cover and cook for a further 5 minutes.
8 When the lentils are tender, put them in a casserole dish; add the other ingredients and mix thoroughly.
9 Cover the casserole, place in the oven; turn the oven off (to conserve fuel) and allow 10 to 15 minutes to heat through before serving.

TO SERVE

This recipe can be used as a basic component of other recipes (some of which follow), or it can be served as the substance of a meal, supplemented by steamed vegetables such as asparagus, broccoli, and cauliflower.

STUFFED ZUCCHINI SURPRISE

For another surprising taste sensation, those overgrown zucchinis or the large vegetable marrows are used. No longer do they have to be merely steamed and served as a somewhat bland vegetable accompaniment to an otherwise tasty meal. This recipe reveals how to actually make them a delicious feature of a cooked meal, using the nutrient-packed, fibre-rich basic recipe on the previous page: Savoury Lentil Surprise.

PREHEAT OVEN TO 150° C (300° F) SERVES 4

INGREDIENTS

1 very large (or 2 medium–large) zucchini
2 tablespoons raw tahini (sesame butter)
½ recipe Savoury Lentil Surprise
1 medium avocado

METHOD

1 The zucchini must first be steamed until it is just tender. It can be cut in half to fit into a steaming saucepan or put into a covered casserole dish for steaming in oven.
2 When it is tender, cut the zucchini lengthwise and remove the seeds.
3 Baste the hollowed centre of the zucchini with tahini.
4 Pack the lentil mix into the zucchini centre(s), using as much as possible and smoothly rounding the top.
5 Place the stuffed zucchinis onto a flat baking tray in the oven to heat through for 15 minutes, and reduce oven temperature to 130° C (265° F).
6 Meanwhile, peel the avocado and cut it in wedges away from stone.
7 Remove the stuffed zucchinis from the oven and decorate the tops with avocado wedges, then serve.

ALTERNATIVES

1 A large vegetable marrow can be used instead of zucchini.
2 A half recipe of Savoury Kasha Casserole can be used instead of Savoury Lentil Surprise.
3 Instead of avocado topping, lightly steamed or sautéed small mushrooms can be used, especially if buckwheat is used, for this recipe does not include as many mushrooms.

TO SERVE

This recipe should be served hot, and it can easily accompany any other recipe in this group. It is also most satisfying served as the centrepiece of the meal with steamed vegetables or with Aubergine Sauce (page 60) or both.

CAPSICUM CAPRICE

Invariably when a vegetarian goes to a quality restaurant and asks for a non-meat dish, the imaginative (?) chef whips up a couple of stuffed capsicums, utilising some savoury rice he has on hand. While the result might be tasty, it is often far from nutritious, for it will focus upon extravagantly spiced white rice. While such spices are often digestive inhibitors, the white rice acts as little more than mere filling when stripped of its nutrient-rich outer covering and bleached. But even unpolished (brown) rice is way down on the list of nutritional grains. So for this recipe, which can be such a bountiful offering, I much prefer to use savoury lentils, relying on the natural flavours of carefully chosen vegetables and herbs for that "little extra something". It is important not to overcook the capsicums, for they are abundant sources of vital vitamin C, which diminishes markedly under intense heat exposure.

PREHEAT OVEN TO 150° C (300° F) SERVES 4

INGREDIENTS

4 large green capsicums
1 small (or ½ large) head cauliflower
½ recipe Savoury Lentil Surprise
8 unbroken half pecan nut kernels

METHOD

1 Carefully cut the entire top off each capsicum, leaving as large an open cup as possible.
2 Wash each capsicum and put it on a flat dish in the oven for 10 minutes.
3 Meanwhile, wash the cauliflower and steam it until just tender (about 15 minutes).
4 Carefully pack the lentil mix into each partly cooked capsicum and return them to the oven for a further 15 to 20 minutes until they are heated through and the capsicums are tender. Smear the oven dish with oil before the final cooking.
5 Decorate each stuffed capsicum top with two pecan nut halves and between each place a small cauliflower floweret (to appear as a tiny tree). Use the remaining cauliflower as the accompanying vegetable.
6 Small pieces of capsicum tops can also be used to decorate top of each stuffed capsicum. They are then ready to serve.

ALTERNATIVES

1 A half recipe of Savoury Kasha Casserole (page 64) can be used instead of lentils.
2 Wedges of avocado can be used on top of each stuffed capsicum instead of pecans.

TO SERVE

The combination of a stuffed capsicum and a portion of steamed cauliflower will provide an appetising meal. Additional steamed vegetables, such as asparagus, beans, or carrots, can also be served. A tossed salad is another nourishing accompaniment to make this a hearty meal.

WHOLEMEAL PASTA PARADISO

Thanks to Italian-born Australians, we now have the ready availability of such foods as zucchini and wholemeal pastas of many different shapes and varieties, none of which were known to us before the Second World War. For some people paradise is a huge plate of spaghetti, macaroni, lasagne or similar, but none could be more nutritionally "paradiso" than the wholemeal version of these pastas. The nutritional difference between these and the white versions made from refined and bleached flour is enormous. Wholemeal pasta is, at best, not as nutritious as the legumes or whole grains used in most of the recipes in this Group, but it is an acceptable occasional alternative when prepared as suggested here with accompaniments selected not only for their flavour but also to balance the nutritional deficiencies of even wholemeal pasta. (Assiduously avoid white pastas, as they contain only one-eighth the fibre of the wholemeal, only half the mineral quantities, and less than a third the B-vitamins, and they are devoid of both vitamins A and C.) Instead of using oil, butter or margarine in tossing the cooked pasta, the highly nutritious sesame butter, tahini, has been used here.

COOK IN OPEN SAUCEPAN; SERVE IN CASSEROLE DISH — SERVES 4

INGREDIENTS

3 litres (10 cups) pure water
1 slice fresh lemon
500 g wholemeal pasta
2 tablespoons chopped fresh chives
2 tablespoons raw tahini

METHOD

1. Bring the water to the boil and add the lemon slice.
2. Gradually add the pasta to the boiling water, ensuring that the water does not go off the boil. Stir occasionally to avoid sticking.
3. Boil the pasta for 15 to 20 minutes until it is tender (duration depends on the pasta's thickness).
4. When the pasta is tender, drain it in a colander. Discard the lemon.
5. Place the pasta in pre-warmed casserole, add the chives and tahini, and toss to mix thoroughly.

TO SERVE

The adaptability of this recipe is almost limitless. It can be served with a wide variety of steamed or sautéed vegetables, such as mushrooms, fresh peas, sweet corn, carrot, beetroot, green beans, asparagus, or cauliflower. It can also be deliciously combined with the previous recipes of Meatless Bolognese Sauce (page 58) or Aubergine Sauce (page 60). Its further adaptability is utilised in the following recipe.

MACARONI EGGPLANT BAKE

The versatility of the eggplant, or aubergine, is superbly utilised here in combination with wholemeal macaroni to provide a delicious meal of valuable nutrients, especially complex carbohydrates and dietary fibre. Two eggplants are prepared in different ways, the larger as a "breaded steak", the other as the basis of a sauce — a most compatible combination.

PREHEAT OVEN TO 150° C (300° F) SERVES 4
Utensils needed: steaming saucepan, large open frypan, covered casserole dish

INGREDIENTS

4 cups pure water
1 slice fresh lemon
200 g wholemeal macaroni
2 tablespoons raw tahini
2 tablespoons chopped fresh chives
500 g fresh green peas in pods
6 small zucchinis
cold-pressed vegetable oil for frying
1 large eggplant
1 large open-range egg, beaten
½ cup raw wheat germ
1 recipe Aubergine Sauce (page 60)

METHOD

1. Bring the water to the boil; add the lemon and macaroni, ensuring that the water does not go off boil. Stir occasionally.
2. Boil the macaroni until tender (about 20 minutes), then drain in a colander.
3. Discard the lemon, place the macaroni in a casserole dish, mix in tahini and chives.
4. Put the casserole in oven to keep warm.
5. Put a flexible steamer stand in saucepan with 1 cm tap water.
6. Bring this water to the boil and add the whole peas; cover and allow to steam for 10 minutes, then add zucchinis to steamer.
7. Steam the vegetables for another 5 minutes until tender.
8. Slice the zucchinis and remove the peas from pods (steaming in pods retains maximum flavour for peas).
9. Cover the bottom of a frypan with oil and heat to just below boiling point.
10. Slice the eggplant (1 cm thick slices); cover the slices with egg then wheat germ, and lightly brown each side in frypan.
11. Empty the macaroni from the casserole into a holding pot (the empty steamer is suitable); arrange a layer of eggplant in bottom of casserole, then a layer of zucchini, covered by half the macaroni. Then arrange the final layer of eggplant, cover with the podded peas, then the rest of the macaroni, and finally top with Aubergine Sauce.
12. Cover the casserole dish, return to the switched off oven to warm in stored heat.

TO SERVE

This is a complete meal. Perhaps only a tossed side salad should be considered if any complement is needed.

GRAND GARBANZO LOAF

Known equally well as the chickpea or garbanzo, this legume is native to southern Europe and Latin America, and it is a special favourite of the Lebanese. It can be used as a whole pea, or ground into flour, or milled into paste (known frequently as hoummus or hummus). In any way, it becomes a very popular food once its characteristic flavour is tasted. Many of us balk at any "new" food and thereby miss a whole new world waiting to be explored. Garbanzo is not new, for the millions who are familiar with its savoury sweetness also benefit from its excellent nutritional properties. The dried peas contain 20 per cent protein, 61 per cent complex carbohydrates (including 5 per cent fibre), plus valuable concentrations of iron, potassium, and niacin (B_3). In this recipe, the garbanzo flavour is captured in a manner that will appeal to both the health conscious and the unadventurous, as a "meat" loaf.

PREHEAT OVEN TO 190° C (375° F) PRESOAK GARBANZOS SERVES 6
Utensils needed: steaming saucepan, small covered frypan, oven loaf dish or tin, large mixing bowl, vegetable juicer

INGREDIENTS

250 g dry garbanzos
500 g fresh carrots
½ cup raw fresh wheat germ
1 teaspoon mixed herbs
2 tablespoons chopped fresh chives
150 g fresh mushrooms, diced
2 medium tomatoes, diced
1 tablespoon cold-pressed vegetable oil
3 large open-range eggs

METHOD

1 Presoak the garbanzos overnight in ample pure water; rinse and continue soaking until ready to cook.
2 Steam the garbanzos until quite tender (30 to 45 minutes), then mash them thoroughly.
3 Wash the carrots and put them through a juicer. Drink the juice to quench your thirst while preparing this saliva-inducing dish.
4 Mix the carrot pulp, wheat germ, mashed garbanzos, herbs, and chives.
5 Lightly sauté the mushrooms and tomatoes in frypan in oil.
6 Add the sautéed mixture and eggs to the garbanzo mixture and mix thoroughly.
7 Pack the mixture into a well-oiled loaf dish, ensuring that no air bubbles remain.
8 Place the dish in the oven; bake until light brown on top (usually 45 minutes).

ALTERNATIVES

1 Sautéed onions can be added to the recipe for extra flavour, although for the discriminating palate, the existing ingredients will suffice.
2 Salt-free powdered vegetable seasoning can be used instead of the mixed herbs.
3 Grated mild cheddar cheese (150 g) can be used instead of the carrot pulp.

TO SERVE

This loaf can be served hot or cold, with steamed vegetables or a tossed salad.

BUTTERNUT CORN HOTPOT

With considerably more dietary fibre than any other variety of pumpkin or potato, butternut pumpkin presents a delightful taste and nutrition treat as the basis of this vegetable casserole. The butternut is also an excellent source of vitamin A, as are carrots and chives, both of which are used in this recipe. The other main vegetable used here is sweet corn, but it should be chosen young and fresh, for then it is also at its sweetest and most easily digested.

PREHEAT OVEN TO 150° C (300° F) SERVES 4

Utensils needed: steaming saucepan, small open frypan, covered casserole dish

INGREDIENTS

4 cobs young sweet corn
600 g butternut pumpkin
3 medium carrots, scrubbed
500 g fresh peas in pod
2 tablespoons raw tahini
2 tablespoons chopped chives
2 medium onions, diced
2 tablespoons cold-pressed vegetable oil
150 g fresh mushrooms, diced
¼ teaspoon ground ginger

METHOD

1 Steam the corn cobs until the kernels are tender (about 15 minutes).
2 Remove the corn; steam the pumpkin, carrots, and peas in their pods.
3 Meanwhile, cut the corn kernels from the cobs, taking care to remove the entire kernel, especially the tiny germ at the head.
4 Put the kernels in a small bowl and mix them with the tahini and chives.
5 As the other vegetables become just tender, remove them from the steamer.
6 Meanwhile sauté the onions in the oil until tender, then add the mushrooms and ginger and sauté a further 5 minutes.
7 Cut the skin from the pumpkin (if wished) and dice or slice as preferred.
8 Slice the carrots and remove the peas from their pods.
9 Place layers of vegetables into a casserole dish, with corn mixture forming a centre layer and the onion mixture poured over top.
10 Cover the casserole dish and put it in the oven until the casserole is thoroughly heated through (about 15 minutes).

ALTERNATIVES

1 Fresh green beans (diced when steamed) can be used instead of peas.
2 Fresh lentil or mung bean sprouts can be added to the casserole dish with the steamed vegetables as the second top layer (under the onions).

TO SERVE

This is a complete main course dish, perhaps requiring no more than a small tossed side salad as accompaniment. It should be served hot from the oven.

GOLDEN BAKED POTATOES

Two Variations on a Favourite Theme

So conditioned are most westerners to the habit of including meat with every meal that little thought is given to a meatless meal in which versatile vegetables comprise the entire main course. Practising vegetarians are exceptions, as they are aware that protein-rich foods are *not* required at every meal. This should help non-vegetarian hostesses from engaging in a painful panic whenever they know guests are non-meat-eaters. The potato recipes here give just a few ways of using a versatile vegetable to provide the desired diversion from meat without the abandonment of flavour. The habitual use of sour cream with baked potatoes is rejected here, in favour of more nutritious, more easily digested natural foods.

WHOLE GREEN AND GOLD POTATOES

PREHEAT OVEN TO 230° C (445° F) SERVES 4

INGREDIENTS

8 medium whole potatoes, scrubbed clean
1 medium avocado, halved and seeded
2 tablespoons raw tahini
1 tablespoon chopped fresh chives
8 sprigs fresh parsley

METHOD

1 Place the whole potatoes at rear of oven to dry bake.
2 After 30 minutes, reduce the oven temperature to 160° C (320° F); leave potatoes to bake until tender (about another 30 minutes).
3 Meanwhile, mash the avocado flesh, then mix in tahini and chives.
4 When the potatoes are tender, remove from the oven and cut them in halves lengthwise.
5 Pack the green avocado mixture onto golden potato halves and top each with a sprig of parsley.

SAVOURY BAKED POTATOES

PREHEAT OVEN TO 200° C (390° F) SERVES 4

INGREDIENTS

4 very large whole potatoes, scrubbed clean
2 tablespoons cold-pressed vegetable oil
½ teaspoon mixed herbs
½ teaspoon powdered salt-free vegetable seasoning (e.g. Dr Jensen's)

METHOD

1 Cut each potato in half lengthwise.
2 Arrange the half potatoes (cut side up) close together on a flat oven tray so they are near the back of the oven when baking.
3 Mix the oil, herbs and seasoning thoroughly together and use the mixture to baste potato faces, retaining a third of the mixture for later use.
4 Put the tray of potatoes in the oven for 30 minutes.
5 Remove the tray from the oven and again baste the potato faces, using the remainder of the oil mixture (ensure it is well mixed).
6 Replace the tray in the oven, and turn the temperature down to 150° C (300° F) to conserve energy.
7 Continue to bake the potatoes until they are tender (usually a further 30 minutes).

TO SERVE

Both variations of Golden Baked Potatoes are prepared and served in their jackets, thereby retaining maximum nourishment. They should be served with a large tossed green salad or with steamed vegetables. If choosing a salad, the ideal basic ingredients are fresh sprouts (particularly alfalfa), celery, cucumber, capsicum, and lettuce. Do not use tomatoes, as they do not combine well with potatoes for good digestion. Suggested steamed vegetables are broccoli, brussels sprouts, and asparagus or carrots.

BUSY PEOPLE'S POTATO CASSEROLE

When preparing natural foods for cooking, the new vegetarian cook is invariably amazed at the simplicity of the process and small amount of cleaning up compared with conventional capers when cooking carnivorously. This recipe is a prime example of delectable vegetarian cookery in its simplest form: it uses only one cooking utensil, requires a mere 20 minutes preparation time, and it can be forgotten while the oven does all the work until eating time. For busy people, it is an ideal meal; for fussy eaters, it is also a most satisfying meal, offering both nutritional and flavour richness. Much of its unique taste derives from the surprisingly effective combination of tahini and yoghurt with these vegetables. The vegetables are sliced to different thicknesses to allow them to cook to similar tenderness together.

PREHEAT OVEN TO 165° C (330° F) SERVES 4

INGREDIENTS

6 medium potatoes, scrubbed
2 medium sweet potatoes, preferably red, scrubbed
1 large eggplant, washed
4 medium zucchinis, washed
2 medium carrots, scrubbed
125 g raw tahini (sesame butter)
2 large onions, peeled and diced
2 teaspoons powdered salt-free vegetable seasoning (e.g. Dr Jensen's)
2 stalks celery, washed and diced
150 g fresh mushrooms, washed and sliced
100 g natural yoghurt (preferably goat's milk)

METHOD

1 Cut potatoes and sweet potatoes lengthwise, then slice them about 3 mm thick; do not peel them.
2 Thinly peel eggplant; cut it into four lengthwise, then slice it in about 4 mm thick pieces.
3 Slice zucchinis about 8 mm thick.
4 Slice carrots about 3 mm thick.
5 Spread a tablespoon of tahini inside the bottom of a large casserole dish, ensuring it is totally covered. Mix the tahini well before use.
6 Arrange in layers half the prepared potato, sweet potato, eggplant, zucchini, and carrot, and sprinkle onion on top.
7 Over these, sprinkle a teaspoon of vegetable seasoning and pour half the remaining tahini.
8 Sprinkle half the celery and mushroom over the tahini, and spread half the yoghurt over these. Do not use flavoured yoghurt.
9 Repeat steps 6, 7 and 8 in order with the rest of the ingredients, by when the casserole dish will be filled.
10 Cover the casserole and place in oven until vegetables are tender (about 1¾ hours). Oven can be turned off after 1½ hours, allowing casserole to cook a further ½ hour in stored heat.

ALTERNATIVES

1 Butternut pumpkin can be used instead of sweet potato.
2 Thinly sliced (2 mm) beetroot can be used instead of one or more carrots.
3 Parsnip can also be used instead of, or as well as, carrots.
4 Other vegetables that lend themselves to use in this versatile recipe (either in addition to or instead of suggested ingredients) are sliced cabbage, fresh green peas, green beans, chokos, Jerusalem artichokes, and marrow.
5 Mixed herbs can be used instead of powdered seasoning.

TO SERVE

As with most of these recipes, this casserole is a complete meal in itself, although a tossed side salad or steamed vegetables (such as broccoli or cauliflower) can provide tasty and nutritious accompaniments.

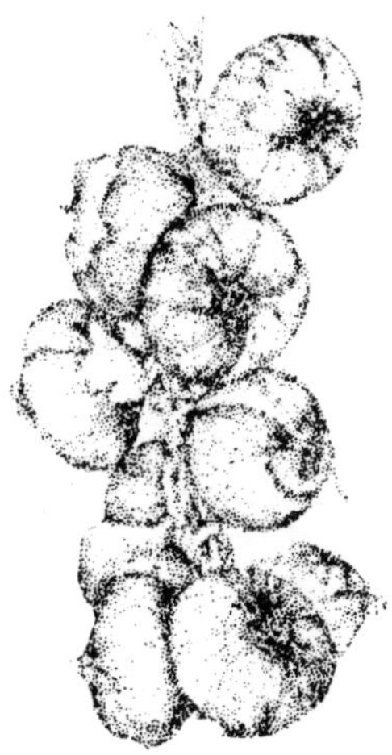

SWEET AND SAVOURY RICE HOTPOT

It will come as something of a disappointment to many people that I place rice so low on the table of nutrient-rich grains. This is especially apparent when it is considered that even dry unpolished rice has a dietary fibre content of only 0.9 per cent and that it offers a meagre 28 mg calcium (per 100 g), yet contains ten times this amount of phosphorus (a decidedly unsatisfactory ratio). However, on the credit side, unpolished rice is a reasonable source of vitamins B_1 and B_3, and an excellent source of the trace mineral (vital for the skin) silicon. But it is the characteristic flavour and texture of rice that have established it as a firm favourite throughout the world. So, for those people who will not be convinced that buckwheat is much better and that rice never need be used, this recipe has been conceived to expand one's versatility with rice, using a crockpot instead of boiling or steaming (if a crockpot is unavailable, refer to Alternatives listed below). And what an exciting new flavour apple juice brings to rice!

PRESET CROCKPOT TO HIGH — SERVES 4

INGREDIENTS

3 cups pure apple juice
250 g unpolished rice
400 g fresh green peas, weighed in pod
4 medium carrots, scrubbed, cut lengthwise and sliced
100 g drained whole black olives
100 g fresh mushrooms, washed and diced
2 tablespoons powdered vegetable seasoning (e.g. Dr Jensen's)
2 tablespoons chopped fresh chives

METHOD

1. Pour the apple juice into the crockpot.
2. When almost boiling, add the rice and stir. Replace the lid.
3. Remove the peas from their pods.
4. After the rice has been cooking for 30 minutes, add peas and carrots and replace the lid.
5. Cook until tender (about 2 hours more).
6. Meanwhile, dice the olives and discard their seeds.
7. Add the mushrooms, olives, seasoning and chives to the crockpot; mix well; replace the lid and turn the temperature control to off.
8. Cook a further 10 minutes in stored heat.

ALTERNATIVES

1. If a crockpot is unavailable, use a large double boiler saucepan with ample tap water boiling in the lower unit. The rice will cook quicker than in a crockpot, but the slower cooking is much more desirable when using apple juice.
2. Mixed herbs can be used instead of powdered seasoning.
3. If a sweet flavour only is preferred, delete the olives, seasoning (or herbs), and chives, and replace them with precooked sweet corn kernels at stage 7.
4. If additional sweetness is desired, add finely grated beetroot at stage 7.

TO SERVE

This can be served as a complete meal or with a side salad or steamed vegetables.

Group 3: Whole Grain Breads

A vast difference exists between the nourishing substance once referred to as "the staff of life" and the rubbery, white loaves given the same name today. Perhaps as the populations of "advanced" countries continue to become more health-conscious, commercial bread manufacturers will abandon the baking of soft, white loaves and turn more to wholesome, wholegrain, unchemicalised breads.

Even so, there is no substitute for fresh, homemade, wholegrain bread. The small amount of time required is an investment in health if bread is demanded in the diet.

There is no doubt that people can exist without bread in their diet. Even the very best bread is a second-rate food in terms of nutritional properties when compared with fresh fruits and vegetables, fresh sprouts, nuts, and seeds. But it cannot be denied, since westerners have lived so long with it as a basic component of their diet, that bread has wide appeal.

I do not intend to dissuade people from the consumption of bread, but rather to encourage them:

1 to reduce their use of bread to the occasional, rather than the regular, and
2 to improve the quality of the bread they consume so that it is the best possible; to achieve this they must make their own bread from the best ingredients, as exemplified by the following recipes.

These recipes all have some vital nutritional factors in common:

1 They include no refined or bleached flour. They use only wholegrain flours, all of which can be ground from the whole grain in the kitchen just before use, ensuring freshness, maximum natural fibre, protein, mineral, and vitamin contents, with minimal oxidation losses.
2 They include no salt or other taste stimulants. This allows the natural flavours of freshly ground grains to be enjoyed and also avoids the risk of digestive or cardio-vascular problems from salt, and the like.
3 They include no artificial sweeteners, or sugar or honey. Naturally sweet foods, such as dried fruits, also add deliciously to texture.
4 They include no chemicals of preservation or colouring. Only fresh or naturally dried ingredients are used, allowing these breads to be kept under refrigeration (in enclosed containers) for many days if needed.
5 They do not rely on wheat as the only bread-baking grain. They utilise the wide variety of flavours, nutritional properties, and textures available from such grains as corn, rice, millet, and, perhaps the tastiest of all grains used in bread baking, rye. Linseed, excellent for sufferers of colonic ailments, can also be used.

Resourceful use of natural foods is made in bread baking, just as it is with other cooked and non-cooked recipes in this book. At the same time, avoidance of the modern habit of extensive aeration of bread induces these loaves to be much heavier, almost "cakey" in some recipes. This returns bread to its original concept: a dense, nourishing, moist, satisfying loaf with sufficient natural flavour and texture to be enjoyably eaten by itself, naked and unspread, if desired.

Many of the nutritional inadequacies associated with the consumption of modern breads are caused by the nature of the spreads chosen to cover that pale, air-laden, parchment-flavoured substance masquerading as bread to make it more palatable. Neither margarine nor butter offer much nutritional virtue, yet they have undesirably high percentages of sodium chloride (common salt), up to a little over 1 per cent in each. Yet, without these, modern breads soon dry out and any other spread added to them often runs through the wide air holes. These other spreads also have potential health risks, being loaded either with white sugar (as in most jams) or salt (as in yeast extracts).

The most nutritious and delicious spreads for bread are avocado (nature's natural spreading fruit) and raw nut or seed butters (or "pastes" as they must be called in Australia to avoid confusion with the dairy apology for a nutritious spread). When these foods are used, they can be applied directly to the bread, as they require no manufactured substance as an intermediary. They are salt-free, and free from hydrogenated and saturated fats and from any added chemicals, as long as one avoids roasted, salted nut butters. My favourites are a mashed blend of avocado and tahini (in equal portions), or raw cashew butter.

In each of the following recipes, stone-ground flour is specified. This is always available from well-stocked health food stores or supermarkets with health food sections. It is more nutritious than steel-milled flour, for in the milling, less heat is generated, thereby minimising any nutrient loss (especially of vitamin B_1) caused by heat. Even better is freshly ground flour; kitchens can be easily equipped with small stone grinders to mill flour from the whole grain just before using it in baking. This also avoids any risk of oxidation, which can lead to rancidity. A few of the more progressive health food stores now possess their own stone grinders and will freshly mill whole grains or seeds for customers while they wait. The improvement in flavour in bread made from freshly milled flour is most noticeable, and these grains also have improved self-raising ability, which will provide a better textured bread.

BUCKWHEAT QUICKBREAD

Here, as in most of the bread recipes in this book, wholewheat flour is a major ingredient. Its bread-making properties put it at the top of the list, even though other flours have superior nutritional properties, particularly buckwheat flour. However, buckwheat flour does not lend itself to sole use in bread making, although it does provide a most desirable supplement to wholewheat, especially in terms of flavour and fibre. In this recipe, the technique of pre-warming the ingredients ensures a speedy method for making a yeast bread, which will save busy people the time required for kneading.

PREHEAT OVEN TO 125° C (255° F) MAKES A 1 KG LOAF

INGREDIENTS

3 cups wholewheat flour
1½ cups buckwheat flour
1 tablespoon (level) dry baker's yeast
2 tablespoons pure maple syrup
1½ cups warm pure water
1 tablespoon cold-pressed vegetable oil

METHOD

1 Pour both the flours into a large mixing bowl and put in a very low oven to warm.
2 Put the dry yeast and maple syrup in separate small containers and also put them in a very low oven to warm at 125° C (255° F).
3 Mix the yeast and maple syrup with half the water in one of the small containers.
4 Make a hollow in the centre of the warm flour and pour in the yeast mixture.
5 Thoroughly mix them together (with hands is best), then add the rest of the water.
6 Ensure all the ingredients are mixed, but there is no need to overwork the mixture.
7 Pour the oil into the bread tin and spread thoroughly over inside surfaces.
8 Pack the dough into a bread tin, leaving a slight hollow in the centre.
9 Place in a pre-warmed warm oven for about 30 minutes to allow preliminary rising, then raise the oven temperature to 180° C (355° F) and bake until the loaf is done (about a further 45 minutes). The oven door must not be opened until baking is complete.
10 Remove the loaf from the oven; use a knife to loosen the bread from the sides of the tin and allow it to stand until cool before removing it from the tin.

ALTERNATIVES

1 To increase sweetness, add more maple syrup or presoaked raisins or sultanas.
2 To make a more spicy loaf, add a teaspoon of cinnamon and half a teaspoon of kelp powder.
3 Another variety can be obtained by reducing the buckwheat and replacing it with half the quantity of wheat germ or linseed flour.

CARROT AND RAISIN RYE BREAD

The fact that most people enjoy sweet spreads on their bread should readily convince commercial bakers to make sweeter loaves. Yet they should achieve this, not with sugar, but with nature's concentrated sweeteners, sun-dried fruits. And there is a simple technique for encouraging these fruits to yield their optimum sweetness: presoak them in pure water (which also plumps the fruit quite deliciously), then use this water in the recipe. Another natural sweetener is carrot pulp, the otherwise wasted residue from juicing carrots. This also adds nourishment and texture to the recipe. Eggs are used for rising instead of yeast in this and a few other recipes, which saves time for the cook and makes a denser bread.

PREHEAT OVEN TO 190° C (375° F) MAKES A 1 KG LOAF

INGREDIENTS

200 g natural raisins
1 cup pure water
700 g fresh carrots
2½ cups wholewheat flour
1½ cups whole rye flour
4 large open-range eggs
½ cup cold-pressed vegetable oil

METHOD

1 Presoak the raisins in the water 1 hour.
2 Wash and trim the ends from the carrots; extract their juice (which you can consume while you prepare this recipe).
3 Collect the carrot pulp and separate it so that it will mix well with flour.
4 In a large mixing bowl, thoroughly mix the carrot pulp and all the flour.
5 Pour the excess water from the raisins into a blender jug.
6 Add the sultanas to the flour mixture and lightly mix them in.
7 Add the eggs and oil to the blender jug, and blend the mixture at medium speed.
8 Pour the blended liquid into the mixing bowl and thoroughly mix until a consistent dough is achieved.
9 Use a tablespoon of oil to spread thoroughly over the inside of a bread tin.
10 Pack the dough mixture into the bread tin, ensuring that no air pockets remain.
11 Bake until the loaf is cooked through, usually 1¾ hours.

ALTERNATIVES

1 A 100 per cent rye loaf can be made if desired, but this is usually too dark in colour and too heavy in texture for most people. By varying the ratio of wholewheat and rye flours, you can achieve the kind of loaf preferred.
2 If using all rye flour, use an additional egg or a large, very ripe banana to help in the raising of the loaf.
3 Sultanas can be used instead of raisins, which suit those palates preferring a firmer fruit.

WHOLEWHEAT FRUIT LOAF

This is the first of two substantial variations of the non-yeast, sweet bread loaf described in the previous recipe. Here a variety of fruits is introduced, with ample alternatives from which to choose for even more variations in flavour. It is a recipe which children, particularly, enjoy — often a double batch has to be made to satisfy those hungry smaller mouths and seemingly bottomless tummies. Using eggs rather than yeast also results in the heavier, more cakey loaf, which gives greater satisfaction to children's appetites.

PREHEAT OVEN TO 190° C (375° F) MAKES A 1 KG LOAF

INGREDIENTS

75 g natural sultanas
75 g natural currants
1 cup pure water
4½ cups wholewheat flour
½ cup cold-pressed vegetable oil
75 g diced sun-dried peaches
4 large open-range eggs
1 large very ripe banana
1 teaspoon cinnamon

METHOD

1 Presoak the sultanas and currants in the water for at least 2 hours.
2 When soaked, drain the excess water from this fruit, and pour it into the blender.
3 Pour the flour and soaked fruit into large mixing bowl; mix well.
4 Add oil, peaches, eggs, banana, and cinnamon to the water in the blender.
5 Blend at medium speed until smooth (about a quarter of a minute).
6 Pour the liquid into the flour mix and thoroughly mix to a dough.
7 Use a tablespoon of oil to spread well over inside of bread tin.
8 Pack the dough mixture into bread tin, ensuring that there are no air pockets.
9 Bake until the loaf is cooked thoroughly, usually 1¾ hours.

ALTERNATIVES

1 Instead of diced peaches, sun-dried apricots (avoid the orangy sulphured variety), dehydrated pineapple or dates can be used.
2 An additional very ripe banana can be used, but dried fruit should be reduced by 75 g (25 g of each variety is suggested).
3 For a variety of flours, one cup of wholewheat flour can be replaced by a cup of rye, buckwheat, rice or corn meal, smoothly ground.

MULTI-GRAIN SWEET BREAD

In this second variation on the non-yeast loaf, carrot pulp is again used, but this time with a variety of flours. Wholewheat is still used as the basis, but it is now supplemented by rye, linseed, and buckwheat. Ripe bananas are used for that special flavour treat, and so is carrot pulp, for this not only improves the texture of any bread, but also provides additional dietary fibre with low kilojoules, plus high vitamin A, with low fat.

PREHEAT OVEN TO 190° C (375° F) MAKES A 1 KG LOAF

INGREDIENTS

150 g natural sultanas
1 cup pure water
500 g fresh carrots
2 cups wholewheat flour
1 cup buckwheat flour
1 cup whole rye flour
½ cup fine linseed meal (flour)
4 large open-range eggs
2 very ripe bananas
½ cup cold-pressed vegetable oil

METHOD

1 Presoak the sultanas in the water for at least 2 hours, preferably overnight.
2 Wash and trim the ends from the carrots, extract their juice (enjoy it while cooking).
3 Collect the carrot pulp in a large mixing bowl, and separate it so that it will mix well in the recipe.
4 Add all the flour to the carrot pulp and mix thoroughly.
5 Pour the excess water from sultanas into a blender jug.
6 Add the sultanas to the flour mixture and lightly mix them in.
7 Add the eggs, bananas, and oil to the blender jug and mix at medium speed for a quarter of a minute.
8 Pour the blended liquid into the flour mixture in the bowl and thoroughly mix until a consistent dough is achieved.
9 Use a tablespoon of oil to spread evenly over the inside of a bread tin.
10 Pack the dough mixture into a bread tin, ensuring that no air pockets remain.
11 Bake until the loaf is cooked through, usually 1¾ hours.

ALTERNATIVES

1 Other flours or meals that can be used instead of rye or linseed are millet, rice, and corn, in equivalent quantities.
2 Natural raisins can be used instead of sultanas; if in a rush, the seeded variety can save time, as they require less soaking (1 hour).
3 If a little spiciness is also sought, add a teaspoon of cinnamon.

WHEATLESS SAVOURY BREAD (Gluten-free)

This recipe has been especially designed for the coeliac disease sufferers, those unfortunate people who have an intolerance to gluten (found abundantly in wheat and rye). Commercial bread is rarely made without some wheat and rye flour, which means that these people must omit bread from their diet, unless they live on a totally natural health diet, in which bread plays no vital role. Most people with coeliac disease resort to rice crackers, but they can easily make themselves a far healthier food, free not only from gluten, but also from sugar, salt, refined carbohydrates, and artificial chemicals.

PREHEAT OVEN TO 190° C (375° F) MAKES A 1 KG LOAF

INGREDIENTS

100 g natural currants
1 cup pure water
500 g fresh carrots
1½ cups fine rice flour
1 cup fine corn meal
½ cup fine linseed meal
½ cup fine buckwheat flour
1 teaspoon cinnamon
1 teaspoon mixed herbs
5 large open-range eggs
½ cup cold-pressed vegetable oil
1 tablespoon hulled sesame seeds (whole)

METHOD

1 Presoak the currants in the water for at least 2 hours, overnight if possible.
2 Wash and trim the ends from the carrots, extract their juice (enjoy it while cooking).
3 Collect the carrot pulp in a large mixing bowl and separate it so that it will mix well in the recipe.
4 Add the flours, cinnamon, and herbs to the carrot pulp and mix thoroughly.
5 Pour the excess water from the currants into a blender jug.
6 Add the currants to the flour mixture and lightly mix them in.
7 Add the eggs and oil to the blender jug and mix at medium speed for 25 seconds.
8 Pour the blended mixture into the flour mixture in the bowl and thoroughly mix until a consistent dough is achieved.
9 Use a tablespoon of oil to spread evenly over the inside of a bread tin.
10 Pack the dough mixture into a bread tin, ensuring that no air pockets remain.
11 Sprinkle the sesame seeds evenly over the top of the dough and lightly push them in.
12 Bake until the loaf is cooked through, usually 1¾ hours.

ALTERNATIVES

1 Some coeliac disease sufferers find even buckwheat flour indigestible, even though it contains less than 1 per cent gluten. It is used here for its nutritional properties and flavour, but it can be replaced by millet meal.
2 If additional sweetness is required, add a ripe banana to the blender or a few sultanas to the currants.

PUMPKIN AND SUNFLOWER BREAD (Gluten-free)

This is a yeasted bread with a vast difference — it is gluten-free and immensely flavoursome, using imaginatively one of nature's most common vegetables, the pumpkin. The fibre-rich properties of butternut pumpkin and the addition of raw sunflower kernels make this a most nutritious bread. It is a speedy recipe to prepare for a yeasted bread and is probably one of the most popular for people who seek optimum nutrition in every meal.

PREHEAT OVEN TO 190° C (375° F) MAKES A 1 KG LOAF

INGREDIENTS

400 g butternut pumpkin, seeds removed
½ cup fine corn meal
½ teaspoon vegetable salt (needed to control yeast in cooking dough)
1 cup cold pure water
1 cup boiling pure water
3 tablespoons warm pure water
1 sachet (7 g) dry baker's yeast
1 tablespoon pure maple syrup
75 g raw sunflower seed kernels
2 cups fine rice flour
½ cup buckwheat flour
½ cup fine millet meal
1 tablespoon cold-pressed vegetable oil (to oil bread tin)
1 tablespoon hulled sesame seeds

METHOD

1 Steam pumpkin until tender, then peel and mash until smooth in a large mixing bowl.
2 In the steaming saucepan, mix the corn meal, salt, and cold water until smooth.
3 Slowly heat the mixture; add the boiling water and stir the mixture until thickened.
4 Remove the corn meal from the heat and allow it to cool.
5 Mix the yeast, warm water, and maple syrup in a separate bowl until smooth.
6 Allow the yeast mixture to stand until the yeast works into double size (10 minutes).
7 Pour the yeast mixture, sunflower seeds, and corn meal into the mixing bowl containing the pumpkin. Mix thoroughly.
8 Add all the flours to the mixture and continue to mix thoroughly for at least 5 minutes.
9 Evenly cover the inside of a bread tin with cold-pressed vegetable oil.
10 Pack the dough into the bread tin, leaving a slight hollow in the centre.
11 Lightly brush surface of dough with oil and sprinkle with sesame seeds.
12 Allow dough to stand for 40 to 45 minutes for initial rising to occur.
13 Place in oven and after 30 minutes reduce temperature to 175° C (345° F).
14 Bake until the loaf is cooked through, for about another hour.

ALTERNATIVES

Wholewheat flour can be used in lieu of rice flour and rye flour can be used in lieu of buckwheat and millet flours if a wheat-rye loaf is required. Alternatively, 3½ cups wholewheat flour will make a completely wheaten loaf.

Opposite top: Savoury Baked Potatoes (see page 73).
Opposite bottom: Raw Salad Sandwich (left) and Avocado and Sprout Sandwich (right) (see page 89).

INDIAN CORN CHAPATI (Gluten-free)

The two oldest religious groups, the Jews and the Hindus, developed similar types of breads back in antiquity, yet there is no record of the two groups learning from each other. Both breads are unleavened and both (the Jewish matzo and the Indian chapati) are becoming quite popular again today. Perhaps the chapati is leading the popularity race with so much interest in Indian culture throughout the west. The chapati is a very simple bread, but it can become rather indigestible to the western stomach if eaten cold. It is designed, therefore, for consumption immediately upon baking, whereas the matzo is more suitable for eating cold. In this recipe, non-gluten flours have been chosen to again provide for the needs of the coeliac sufferers, although the resultant chapatis will be enjoyed by all.

COOK ON SKILLET | MAKES 6 CHAPATIS

INGREDIENTS

3 cups corn (maize) meal
1 cup fine rice flour
1 teaspoon salt-free powdered vegetable seasoning (e.g. Dr Jensen's)
1 cup pure water
3 tablespoons cold-pressed corn oil

METHOD

1 Thoroughly mix the flours and seasoning.
2 Mix the water and oil together either by vigorous shaking or, more easily, in the blender.
3 Gradually add the liquid to the flour, taking care that the dough does not become too sticky.
4 Thoroughly knead the dough for 2 to 3 minutes until smooth.
5 Divide the dough into six equal portions.
6 Roll the pieces of dough flat, or press them flat with the palms of the hands.
7 Place portions of dough on a dry skillet over a moderately hot heat (on stove hotplate or over an open fire).
8 Cook until brown on underside, then turn over and repeat.

ALTERNATIVES

1 Any of the vast varieties of flour available can be used in this recipe. Buckwheat flour with rye makes a delicious combination, but it is not gluten-free.
2 A mashed banana can be used instead of seasoning for a sweeter flavour.

TO SERVE

Serve the chapatis immediately they are cooked. Use as spreads tahini, raw nut butters or avocado. A mashed mixture of equal parts of avocado and tahini, topped with alfalfa sprouts, makes a delicious meal.

Opposite top: Carrot and Raisin Rye Bread (see page 80).
Opposite bottom: Muesli Muffins (see page 86).

MUESLI MUFFINS

Developed by the famed Bircher-Benner Health Clinic of Zurich, Switzerland, muesli has become synonymous with thoughts of a healthy cereal breakfast. Essentially a mixture of coarsely ground whole grains, flaked grains, nut pieces, and sun-dried fruits, muesli offers an excellent basis for the baking of some of the tastiest and most nutritious muffins imaginable. Toasted muesli should not be used if you want optimum nourishment from this recipe; using raw muesli (such as found in health food stores) avoids nutritional losses from extensive double cooking. The use of soya milk also avoids any problems that might arise from intolerance to animal milks.

PREHEAT OVEN TO 190° C (375° F) MAKES 24 MUFFINS

INGREDIENTS

2 cups wholewheat flour
1 cup whole rye flour
2 cups raw muesli
½ cup pure water
½ cup cold-pressed vegetable oil
3 tablespoons pure maple syrup
2 tablespoons instant soya milk powder
4 large open-range eggs
2 medium very ripe bananas

METHOD

1 In a large mixing bowl, thoroughly mix the flours and muesli.
2 Blend together at medium speed the water, oil, maple syrup, soya milk powder, eggs and bananas.
3 Combine the liquid with the dry ingredients, mixing thoroughly. (As different brands of muesli vary in constituency, the mixture could need a little extra flour if it is too moist, or extra water if it is too dry.)
4 Put the mixture in well-oiled cups of a muffin tin or shape into muffins on a well-oiled flat tray.
5 Bake the muffins until cooked through, about 20 to 30 minutes depending on muffin size.

ALTERNATIVES

1 For a sweet alternative to water, pure apple or pear juice can be used, in which case maple syrup will not be required.
2 A variety of other flours can replace rye, such as buckwheat, rice or millet. To convert these into gluten-free muffins, replace the wholewheat flour with rice flour and rye with millet or corn.
3 If additional fruitiness is desired, use 100 g natural sultanas and presoak them in the water. This eliminates the need for maple syrup and the muesli should be reduced to 1½ cups.

Group 4: The Health Sandwich

There is no disputing that sandwiches fill the stomach and provide a long feeling of satiety. But they are rarely composed of wholesome constituents and could never be considered as ideal combinations for the digestion.

School, college or office lunches would be nutritionally far superior if composed of fresh fruit or vegetables. It is a simple matter to pack a prepared whole salad for the midday meal, which can either be eaten in its uncut state or prepared into a tossed salad. An alternative is a midday meal of apples and pears with bananas and dates or other suitable fruit combinations. Such a meal is easily prepared and is much more nutritious and sustaining than the average run of sandwiches. And this meal is ideal for anyone seeking to trim a little excess weight from their body.

Two hundred years ago, the midday meal was considered the most important of the day. Even today, many Europeans maintain this tradition and allocate a siesta time afterwards to "sleep off" their heavy gastronomical indulgence. But the 4th Earl of Sandwich (1718–1792) inadvertently changed all this, with no small nudging from the Industrial Revolution. Both forces sought to minimise the time taken to comfortably consume a nutritious midday meal. A compromise was achieved by which workers could stay longer at their monotonous machines, on the one hand, and by which the aristocracy could continue uninterruptedly at their gaming tables, on the other. Greed festered behind both developments, led by the invention of the "portable meal" of a piece of meat or vegetable, covered top and bottom by a slice of buttered bread. John Montagu Sandwich (after whom the Sandwich Islands — later Hawaii — were named when he was First Lord of the Admiralty in 1778) was credited with this invention, for he would otherwise never have abandoned the gaming tables. Modern usage has ensured that this aristocrat's name has become one of the best known in history. However, his famous midday snack continues to do him no more credit than the purpose of its invention, for it generally remains today as one of compromising convenience, rather than fulfilling nutritional needs. It is an accepted convention that commands considerable allegiance.

Most children and adults like to feel "part of the group". Children are especially responsive to the dictates of their peer group, for whom convention is secure and comfortable. The wise parent will consider these needs by providing intelligent "compromises" in the form of health sandwiches. These will comprise nutritional foods, suitably combined for best digestion, held within two slices of wholesome, homemade bread. The following sandwich suggestions are intended as general guides for creative parents. They use natural foods in their most convenient forms, such as raw nut butters, tahini or avocado for spreads; even steamed mashed potato, pumpkin or lentils can be used, as long as the bread is naturally moist and wrapped well to exclude air. Salad vegetables incontestably offer the most nutritious and varied form of filling. Who would again buy a shop-made sandwich?

Each of the following sandwich recipes can be used with any type of bread, but one of the homemade breads from the last group of recipes will be greatly preferred by the taste buds. Each recipe is for one complete sandwich, and it can be easily multiplied for multiple sandwiches. Many people prefer to have their bread lightly toasted before making into a sandwich; there is no nutritional objection to this, in fact, often a light toasting will improve a bread's digestibility. Each of these recipes can be converted to an "open sandwich" by simply using only one slice of bread for each set of ingredients.

It is intended that these sandwich ideas be general guidelines, for they give rise to a vast variety of creative sandwich ideas in the use of many delicious natural food alternatives. Note that tomatoes are not recommended for sandwiches, for they do not digestively combine well with starch.

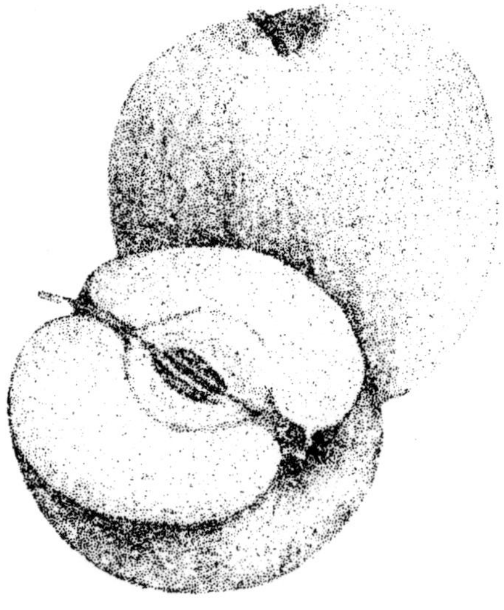

RAW SALAD SANDWICH

INGREDIENTS
½ small celery stalk, finely chopped
½ small carrot, finely grated
1 tablespoon alfalfa sprouts
1 small mushroom, finely chopped
½ teaspoon chopped parsley
¼ teaspoon Instant Fresh Mayonnaise (page 30)
2 lettuce leaves
½ teaspoon raw tahini
2 slices homemade bread

METHOD
1 Mix the celery, carrot, sprouts, mushroom, and parsley with the mayonnaise.
2 Spread the tahini on one side of each slice of bread.
3 Lay lettuce leaves over tahini-spread bread faces.
4 Place salad on one bread face and cover with second.
5 Cut into two or four as required.

AVOCADO AND SPROUT SANDWICH

INGREDIENTS
½ small avocado
¼ teaspoon chopped chives
2 slices homemade bread
1 heaped tablespoon alfalfa sprouts

METHOD
1 Mash the avocado and mix the chives into it.
2 Spread the avocado mash onto one face of each slice of bread.
3 Place sprouts onto one bread face and cover with second.
4 Cut into two or four as required.

COOL GREEN SANDWICH

INGREDIENTS
½ small avocado
1 tablespoon raw tahini
¼ teaspoon chopped chives
2 slices homemade bread
¼ small green cucumber, diced
¼ small green capsicum, diced

METHOD
1 Mash the avocado and mix into it the tahini and chives.
2 Spread this mixture over one face of each slice of bread.
3 Mix the cucumber and capsicum and spread them on one of the spread faces.
4 Bring both slices of bread together to make the sandwich and cut to suit.

ABC HEALTH SANDWICH

INGREDIENTS
2 spears fresh Asparagus
½ small Avocado
2 slices homemade bread
¼ small raw Beetroot, finely grated
½ small Carrot, finely grated
½ teaspoon chopped parsley

METHOD
1 Steam the asparagus until tender, then chop and mash.
2 Mash the avocado and spread onto one face of each slice of bread.
3 Mix the beetroot, carrot and parsley together and spread onto one face of bread.
4 Spread the asparagus onto the other bread face.
5 Bring both slices of bread together and cut the sandwich into desired size.

CELERY AND SULTANA SANDWICH

INGREDIENTS
½ small avocado
2 slices homemade bread
½ small celery stalk, finely chopped
1 tablespoon natural sultanas

METHOD
1 Mash the avocado and spread it on one face of each slice of bread.
2 Mix the celery and sultanas and spread on the one bread face.
3 Bring the bread slices together and cut the sandwich into desired size.

SAVOURY POTATO SANDWICH

INGREDIENTS
1 small potato, scrubbed clean
½ small avocado
1 tablespoon raw tahini
½ teaspoon chopped chives
2 slices homemade bread
1 small mushroom, finely chopped

METHOD
1 Steam the potato until tender.
2 Mash the potato and avocado and mix them together.
3 Mix in the tahini and chives, to form a smooth paste.
4 Spread the paste onto one face of each slice of bread.
5 Sprinkle the mushroom on one face and cover with the other slice of bread.
6 Cut the sandwich into desired size.

SPROUTED LENTIL SANDWICH

INGREDIENTS
1 tablespoon sprouted lentils
½ tablespoon raw tahini
1 small mushroom, finely chopped
½ teaspoon chopped parsley
½ small avocado
2 slices homemade bread

METHOD
1 Lightly chop lentils, then mix them with the tahini, mushroom and parsley.
2 Mash the avocado and spread it on one face of each slice of bread.
3 Cover one face of bread with the lentil mixture.
4 Bring bread faces together and cut the sandwich into desired size.

PEANUT BUTTER AND CELERY SANDWICH

INGREDIENTS
½ small celery stalk, finely chopped
½ teaspoon chopped parsley
1 tablespoon unsalted peanut butter (preferably raw)
2 slices homemade bread

METHOD
1 Mix the celery and parsley together.
2 Spread the peanut butter on one face of each slice of bread.
3 Sprinkle the celery mixture onto one bread face.
4 Bring the bread faces together and cut the sandwich into desired size.

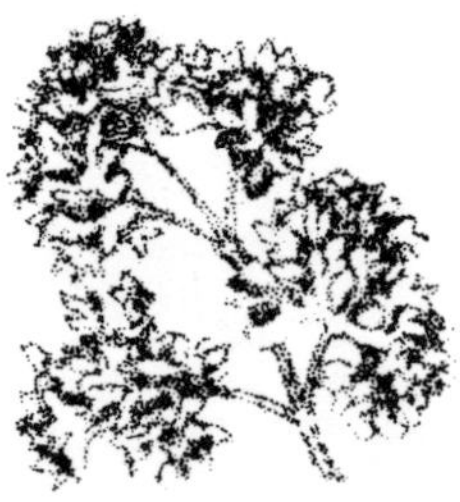

SAVOURY LENTIL SANDWICH

INGREDIENTS
1 large lettuce leaf
½ small avocado
2 slices homemade bread
1 tablespoon Savoury Lentil Surprise (page 65)

METHOD
1 Finely shred the lettuce.
2 Spread the avocado on one face of each slice of bread.
3 Spread the lentil mix onto one bread face and cover with lettuce.
4 Bring the sandwich slices together and cut into desired size.

MAGIC MACARONI SANDWICH

INGREDIENTS
½ tablespoon raw peanut butter (or raw tahini)
2 slices homemade bread
1 tablespoon Wholemeal Pasta Paradiso (page 68)
1 tablespoon fresh alfalfa sprouts

METHOD
1 Spread the peanut butter on one face of each slice of bread.
2 Spread the macaroni on one bread face and cover with sprouts.
3 Bring the sandwich slices together and cut into desired size.

GARBANZO LOAF SANDWICH

INGREDIENTS
1 tablespoon raw tahini
2 slices homemade bread
1 slice Grand Garbanzo Loaf (page 70)
1 small carrot, grated finely
¼ teaspoon Instant Fresh Mayonnaise (page 30)

METHOD
1 Spread the tahini on one face of each slice of bread.
2 On one bread face, place a slice of garbanzo loaf.
3 Mix the grated carrot with mayonnaise.
4 Cover the garbanzo slice with the carrot mixture.
5 Bring the sandwich slices together and cut into desired size.

CASHEW AND CAPSICUM SANDWICH

INGREDIENTS
¼ red capsicum, diced finely
1 lettuce leaf, finely shredded
1 tablespoon raw unsalted cashew butter
2 slices homemade bread

METHOD
1 Mix the capsicum and lettuce together.
2 Spread the cashew butter on one face of each slice of bread.
3 Sprinkle the capsicum mixture onto one bread face.
4 Bring the bread faces together and cut the sandwich into desired size.

BANANA AND CASHEW SANDWICH

INGREDIENTS
1 tablespoon raw unsalted cashew butter
2 slices homemade bread
½ ripe medium banana

METHOD
1 Spread the cashew butter on one face of each slice of bread.
2 Slice the banana onto one bread face.
3 Bring the bread faces together and cut the sandwich into desired size.

CAUTION
As banana tends to oxidise quickly, do not add it to the bread until the sandwich is ready to be eaten. For school lunches, send two cashew butter sandwiches and a whole banana, which is eaten from the hand with each mouthful of sandwich, rather than sliced onto it.

BANANA AND DATE SANDWICH

This sandwich should only be made immediately before being eaten; owing to the tendency of banana to rapidly oxidise, it is not suited for school lunches.

INGREDIENTS
5 sun-dried whole dates
½ tablespoon currants (or sultanas)
½ ripe medium banana
2 slices homemade bread

METHOD
1 Remove the seeds and dice the dates into small pieces.
2 Mix the date pieces and currants (or sultanas).
3 Mash the banana and spread it over one face of each slice of bread.
4 Sprinkle the fruit mixture onto one open face.
5 Bring the bread faces together and cut the sandwich into desired size.

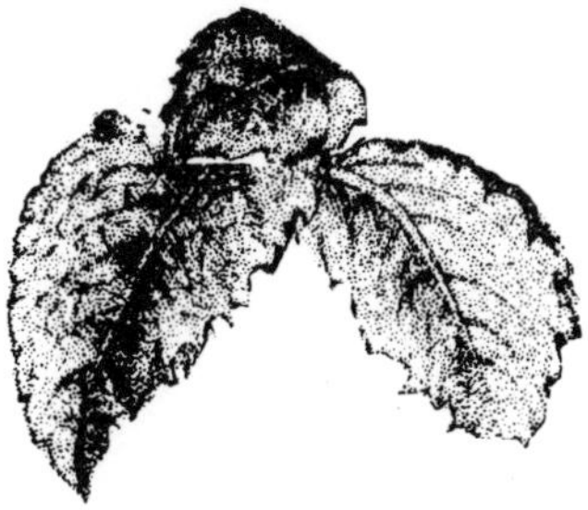

Group 5: Sweets and Celebration Specialties

It is time to say that children love sweets — children of all ages, from 1 to 100. It seems that the older we grow, the greater is the temptation to indulge in sweets. With a little care and understanding we can enjoy these occasional indulgences without risking indigestion, increasing the waistline, or ruining our teeth.

Some of the sweetest foods available are also some of the healthiest. Rich in minerals and natural energy-producing sugars are sun-dried dates, raisins, apricots, figs, prunes, dried bananas and dried pineapple, for instance. Sun-dried or dehydrated fruits should always be preferred to brightly coloured sulphured or caustic-dipped fruits from commercial mass producers. Natural drying guarantees greater natural sweetness and higher nutritional properties.

Sun-dried fruits provide an excellent basis for flavouring cakes, biscuits, and desserts. Because of their highly concentrated sweetness, they are best eaten by themselves or with fresh non-acid fruits. Take special care to avoid combining concentrated protein foods (such as nuts, seeds, cheese, eggs, meat or fish) with sweets in the same meal, otherwise gastric indigestion (from belching to distension or headaches) could result. For further guidance on combining foods for health, refer to my complete health manual, *New Dimensions in Health* (Angus & Robertson Publishers, 1983).

The most natural non-acidic sweetener is pure maple syrup. By tapping certain varieties of North American maple trees, the sap is collected, then concentrated by the evaporation of half its natural moisture content. The resultant liquid is pure maple syrup. (Avoid the cheaper maple syrups that are diluted with corn or cane syrups.)

While honey is a natural product and is much more acceptable than cane sugar, it is, nevertheless, quite acidic, whereas pure maple syrup is a natural sweetener with a neutral pH, similar to that of water. Admittedly, pure maple syrup is more expensive than pure honey, but its nutritional advantages more than justify the investment.

Recommended natural sweeteners in the following recipes are sun-dried fruits and pure maple syrup. However, if personal preferences dictate the use of honey, it can be substituted on those occasions when maple syrup is listed, but it is no substitute for dried fruits. (As honey contains about 19 per cent water and maple syrup contains about 33 per cent, honey is the more concentrated sweetener, so when using it instead of maple, reduce the recommended quantity by one-third.) For your health's sake, never substitute refined sugar or any other form of cane sugar or beet sugar or corn syrup — unless, of course, you are especially fond of the local dentist or physician!

In many cases, the recipes for sweets are among the simplest in this book. This is due to an intelligent recognition of the inherent sweetness in so many natural foods and its capturing by way of simple application and combination. As throughout life, so often the simplest things are the most enjoyable!

PENGUIN ICE CREAM

There is little doubt that the most universally popular sweet today is ice cream. But the commercially produced confections bearing this name can be a danger to community health. *Choice* magazine of January 1983 has at last revealed to the public what many nutritionists have been saying for years — that commercial ice creams contain too many chemicals (in some cases up to 22), too much refined sugar (averaging 20 per cent), too much saturated fat, and too little food value. As many people have allergic reactions to artificial substances in food, ice cream can become a danger unless one has a nutritious recipe for a homemade ice cream that is also a food. And here it is. This is a smooth, creamy, nourishing ice cream that uses no animal products (soya milk is used); it can be made in five minutes; and it is much more nutritious than any commercially available ice creams. This is a basic recipe; flavour and texture variations are found in the following recipe.

NO COOKING REQUIRED
BLENDING AND FREEZING ONLY REQUIRED

MAKES 1 LITRE (4½ CUPS)

INGREDIENTS

4 heaped tablespoons instant soya milk powder
1 tablespoon lecithin powder or granules
4 large very ripe bananas
4 tablespoons pure maple syrup
1 cup cold-pressed vegetable oil (safflower or sunflower preferred)
1 cup pure water

METHOD

1 Put in the blender jug in order: soya milk powder, lecithin, bananas, maple syrup, oil, and water.
2 Blend at top speed until smooth (about half a minute).
3 Pour into suitable refrigerator container, cover, and put in the freezer. The ice cream will set firmly in 6–8 hours.

NOTE

As the natural ice creams in this group are so attractive, show them off by choosing a clear refrigerator container, for this can then also act as an attractive serving container. This ice cream does not require a second blending. It will freeze in a few hours, although this will take longer if the container is deep. Should it ever thaw, this ice cream can be refrozen without any flavour or nutritional loss, for it has no artificial chemicals to start an interreaction (as occurs in commercial ice creams, which must be thrown out if they thaw — imagine what happens when they thaw in your stomach!).

TO SERVE

In company with any other sweet, with a fresh fruit salad (excluding acid fruits, which do not mix well with sweet fruits in the stomach) or served on its own, this ice cream is a winner. And because it is not aerated, it will be consumed in smaller quantities than commercial ice creams, further justifying the higher expense of its nutritious ingredients.

CAROB AND SULTANA ICE CREAM

From the basic ice cream recipe (Penguin Ice Cream, page 97), a few variations can be made, by which both texture and flavour take on new dimensions of deliciousness. By the addition of carob, with its chocolate-like flavour, and of sultanas and their sweet chewiness, this ice cream becomes even more nutritious. Carob increases the calcium content, while the sultanas reinforce the vital iron, potassium, and B-vitamins already to be found in a good instant soya milk powder. Rarely can a dessert be accorded such complimentary nutritional comments.

NO COOKING REQUIRED
BLENDING AND FREEZING ONLY REQUIRED
PRESOAKING OF SULTANAS REQUIRED

MAKES 1 LITRE (4½ CUPS)

INGREDIENTS

100 g natural sultanas
1 cup pure water
4 heaped tablespoons instant soya milk powder
2 tablespoons fine carob powder
1 tablespoon lecithin powder or granules
3 large very ripe bananas
3 tablespoons pure maple syrup
1 cup cold-pressed vegetable oil

METHOD

1 Presoak the sultanas in the water for at least 2 hours, overnight if possible.
2 Place in a blender jug in order: soya milk powder, carob, lecithin, bananas, maple syrup, oil, and the water drained from the sultanas.
3 Blend at top speed until smooth (about half a minute).
4 Pour into suitable refrigerator container, preferably a clear one.
5 Sprinkle sultanas over the liquid and mix them in.
6 Cover the container and put it in the freezer. This ice cream will set in 6–8 hours.

ALTERNATIVES

1 Instead of sultanas, sun-dried dates or seeded raisins can be used. They do not require presoaking, but they should be diced into small pieces before mixing them into the liquid.
2 Another alternative to sultanas is dehydrated pineapple. This will need to be presoaked and cut into small pieces too.
3 A further alternative to sultanas is prunes, but caution should be exercised with these as they can be quite cathartic to some people. If choosing them, use only 50 g and presoak, then dice.

TO SERVE

Serve as Penguin Ice Cream recipe (page 97).

MAPLE BAKED CUSTARD

Second only to ice cream as a favourite sweet is the custard. The word first came into use as far back as 1450, deriving from the French word used to describe a baked mixture of eggs beaten with milk and sweetening. Indeed, the thick, rich creaminess of a baked custard is universally popular, whether served hot or cold. But health-conscious people need not avoid such a favourite because it has become the traditional combination of refined cane sugar, pasteurised cows' milk, and battery-laid eggs. The following recipe is a basic guide to making a baked custard that is a healthy occasional treat for young and old. This recipe can be easily adapted to almost infinite variations of custards and puddings, as a few further recipes will reveal. In this basic recipe, soya milk, pure maple syrup, and open-range fresh eggs are the main ingredients, the combination of which offers an excellent range of nutritional properties, including protein, calcium, phosphorus and iron.

PREHEAT OVEN TO 150° C (300° F) BLENDING REQUIRED SERVES 8

INGREDIENTS

6 tablespoons instant soya milk powder
3 cups pure water
4 tablespoons pure maple syrup
4 large open-range eggs

METHOD

1 Blend all the ingredients.
2 Pour them into an open casserole dish.
3 Stand the dish in a larger tray in hot water.
4 Bake until just set (about 1½ hours).

ALTERNATIVES

1 The addition of 100 g dates to the blending mixture will increase sweetness and allow a reduction in maple syrup to half.
2 The addition of 100 g natural sultanas (presoaked in a cup of the water) will also allow a reduction of maple syrup to half. The sultanas should not be blended but added to liquid in dish.
3 A sprinkling of ground cinnamon or nutmeg on top is highly palatable to many.

TO SERVE

This custard should be allowed to complete setting as it cools after removal from the oven. It can then be served at room temperature or from the refrigerator (where it should be stored). It is quite delicious on its own, or served with some of the forthcoming recipes, such as Baked Fruit Duet (page 104).

BUTTERNUT BAKED CUSTARD

By now my readers will have recognised that I am rather fond of butternut pumpkin. This preference is not emotional; it is based on the two aspects of food that should always be equally considered — taste and nutrients. The sweet, creamy texture of butternut pumpkin lends itself to a vast variety of uses in cooking, while its fibre-richness and attractive vitamin–mineral analyses (especially vitamin A) mark it as one of the top vegetables on the nutritional table. It is unusual to find it in a custard recipe, and the same can be said for ricotta cheese, which is also one of my favourites among dairy products. It is here used instead of milk and makes for an especially creamy and smooth custard.

PREHEAT OVEN TO 150° C (350° F) BLENDING AND STEAMING REQUIRED SERVES 8

INGREDIENTS

750 g butternut pumpkin, seeds removed
½ cup pure water
½ cup pure maple syrup
½ teaspoon ground cinnamon
4 large open-range eggs
500 g fresh ricotta cheese
½ teaspoon ground nutmeg

METHOD

1 Steam the butternut until it is tender, then remove skin and mash.
2 Into the blender, place in order: water, maple syrup, cinnamon, pumpkin, eggs, and the ricotta cheese cut into pieces.
3 Blend at three-quarters of full speed until smooth (about half a minute).
4 Pour into an open casserole dish and sprinkle nutmeg on top.
5 Stand the dish in hot water in a larger tray.
6 Bake until it is just set (about 1¼ hours).

ALTERNATIVES

1 If a sweeter dessert with some chewiness is wanted, 100 to 150 g dried fruits can be added to mixture when it is poured into casserole. Choose from sultanas, raisins or currants (all of which should be presoaked, and use this water for the 3 tablespoons listed), chopped dates or dehydrated pineapple, sun-dried apricots or peaches.
2 If fresh ricotta cheese is not readily available, natural cottage cheese can be used instead.

TO SERVE

Serve as Maple Baked Custard (page 99).

Opposite: Yoghurt Whirl Parfait (see page 105).

BAKED FRUIT CUSTARD

A variation on the recipe High-Protein Custard (page 54) can be made by replacing nuts, lecithin, and yeast with bananas, dried fruits, and cinnamon. This results in a sweet baked custard, which is ideal either as a dessert or as a meal in itself. The basic ingredients of soya milk powder and eggs remain unchanged, resulting in a similar custard, but one that is higher in energy-producing natural sugars. This, of course, also makes it somewhat less desirable to anyone with a weight problem.

PREHEAT OVEN TO 150° C (300° F) BLENDING REQUIRED SERVES 8

INGREDIENTS

5 tablespoons instant soya milk powder
4 cups pure water
4 large fresh open-range eggs
2 large ripe bananas, peeled
125 g natural sultanas
125 g sun-dried dates, pitted
1 teaspoon ground cinnamon
sprinkle ground nutmeg

METHOD

1 Blend all the ingredients (except the nutmeg) together in blender at three-quarters of full speed. It is generally necessary to blend in two stages, using half the ingredients at a time.
2 Pour the mixture into a large deep casserole dish; sprinkle with nutmeg.
3 Stand the casserole dish in a larger, flatter, ovenware dish that is half full of hot water.
4 Put dishes into the oven; do not cover.
5 After baking for 15 minutes, reduce the oven temperature to 120° C (250° F).
6 Bake until just set, about 1½ hours total time.

ALTERNATIVES

1 If sultanas are desired whole, presoak them until they are plump, using some of the soaking water as part of the total 4 cups.
2 Raisins can be used instead of either dates or sultanas, or as well, if additional sweetness is desired. They can be either presoaked for whole plumpness or they can be blended with mixture.

TO SERVE

As a meal on its own, or with fresh fruit, this baked custard will be found most delicious if baked the day before it is required. When it is cool, store it in the refrigerator and serve cold. Even though it contains no added sweetener, it will be found to be a deliciously sweet food.

Opposite top: Penguin Ice Cream (see page 97).
Opposite bottom: Californian Date Pie (see page 107).

BAKED ALMOND PUDDING

For growing youths, active sportspeople, vigorous workers, and anyone else with a need for increased dietary protein intake, this pudding offers a delicious answer. Not an ingredient used in this pudding is without a reasonable concentration of valuable protein (except the water and maple syrup). Although maple syrup has but a trace of protein, it is a very good source of calcium, a nutritional companion of protein.

PREHEAT OVEN TO 130° C (265° F) BLENDING REQUIRED SERVES 6

INGREDIENTS

2 tablespoons instant soya milk powder
125 g fine blanched almond meal
2 tablespoons lecithin powder or granules
1 tablespoon powdered nutritional yeast (brewer's or torula)
4 large open-range eggs
4 tablespoons pure maple syrup
3½ cups pure water

METHOD

1 Place in blender jug all ingredients as they are in the above order.
2 Blend thoroughly at three-quarters of full speed for about half a minute.
3 Pour into a large open casserole dish.
4 Stand the dish in hot water in a larger tray.
5 Bake until just set (about 2 hours). This pudding is intentionally cooked for longer than usual at the lower temperature to better preserve protein quality.

ALTERNATIVES

1 Instead of almond meal, whole natural almonds can be used, but first they must be skinned, dried, and ground into a fine meal. This is the more nutritious way.
2 Cashew meal can be used instead of almond; it is made by grinding raw cashew pieces into a fine meal in an electric coffee grinder or similar.
3 For anyone with an intolerence to yeast, an extra tablespoon of soya milk powder can be used instead.

TO SERVE

This is a complete meal in itself. By nature of its extreme richness, it would not nutritionally combine well with any other food in the same meal.

GOLDEN RICE PUDDING

Traditionally, no dessert section of a recipe book is complete without a rice pudding. But usually such puddings are far from nutritious, being prepared from boiled refined white rice, sweetened with refined white sugar (or honey, by slightly more aware cooks), flavoured with a pinch of refined white salt, and swimming in a sea of pasteurised white cow's milk. Not a pretty scene from the nutritional viewpoint! So in the interests of improved health and taste, this recipe dares to be different. Maximum nourishment is retained in the rice when it is steamed in a double boiler and when only whole, unpolished rice is used. Only the natural sweetness of naturally dried fruits is used, which provides the golden glow. Highly nutritious, easily digested, allergy-free soya milk is far more suited to human consumption than animal milks. Finally, salt (with all its inherent problems for health) is not needed to "bring out the flavour", because the flavour is not lost to refining or poor cooking methods.

PREHEAT OVEN TO 135° C (275° F) SERVES 8

Utensils required: double boiler saucepan, blender, open casserole dish

INGREDIENTS

150 g natural sultanas
6 cups pure water
250 g unpolished (brown) rice
3 large open-range eggs
100 g pitted dates
6 tablespoons instant soya milk powder
½ teaspoon nutmeg

METHOD

1 Presoak the sultanas in 3 cups of water for at least 2 hours.
2 Place the other 3 cups of water in the top of a double boiler and add the rice, with water boiling in lower saucepan.
3 Cover the double boiler and cook the rice until it is tender (about 1 hour).
4 Drain the water from the sultanas into a blender jug and add the eggs, dates, and soya milk powder (which should be in bottom of jug).
5 Blend the mixture until smooth; use three-quarters of full speed for about half a minute.
6 Pour the cooked rice into a casserole dish, add the sultanas and the blended liquid and mix them together well.
7 Stand the casserole dish in hot water in a larger tray. Sprinkle with nutmeg.
8 Cook until just set (about 1½ hours).

ALTERNATIVES

1 Instead of sultanas, raisins or currants or a mixture of any can be used.
2 For varied flavour, use pure maple syrup (¼ cup) instead of dates.
3 Another flavour variation is obtained by using 2 tablespoons of carob powder as well as any of the above suggestions.

BAKED FRUIT DUET

In the following recipe for whole baked fruit use is made of the excellent baking qualities of granny smith apples and whole bananas in their skins. It is one of the simplest recipes ever devised—and simply delicious. Granny Smith was indeed a real person who lived in the Sydney suburb of Ryde over a century ago. It was in the 1870s that she accidentally happened upon the unique variety of hard, green apple that today bears her name and is becoming famous throughout the world for its excellent storage properties and crisp sweetness.

PREHEAT OVEN TO 175° C (345° F) SERVES 4

INGREDIENTS

4 large granny smith apples
12 sun-dried whole dates
2 tablespoons pure maple syrup
4 large ripe bananas

METHOD

1 Remove the seeds from dates, and chop the dates into small pieces.
2 Put the maple syrup into a small bowl and add the dates. Mash the two together.
3 Scrub the apples and remove their cores; leave the skins on.
4 Stuff the date mixture into the centres of the apples.
5 Wrap the apples in aluminium foil and stand them in a shallow baking dish, leaving room for bananas to be added.
6 Put in the oven for 20 minutes to allow for advanced cooking.
7 Add the whole bananas to the baking tray after the apples have cooked for 20 minutes. Ensure that the banana skins have not been broken.
8 Bake for a further 5 minutes, then turn the oven off.
9 Keep in oven until the banana skins turn deep black (about another 30 minutes).

NOTE

This cooking can be taking place while the main coarse of the meal is being consumed, ensuring its readiness in time for the serving of the dessert. This recipe can also be deliciously and conveniently prepared in the charcoal of a barbecue. The only modification is the wrapping of the bananas in aluminium foil too; put the apples and bananas in the fire's embers to cook, but ensure that each fruit is thoroughly wrapped in the foil.

TO SERVE

This dessert should not be served after a meal in which concentrated protein foods have been served if optimum digestion is desired. It is best served after a meal of baked potatoes and vegetables, or a large green salad.

YOGHURT WHIRL PARFAIT

The popularity of yoghurt is now undoubted. Up to twenty years ago, only a minority of people had included yoghurt in their diet. Since then it has been widely recognised that yoghurt is an excellent means by which to enjoy milk protein in a manner the human stomach can readily metabolise (for this is the major nutritional benefit of yoghurt), and more and more people are including it in their dietary habits. As the basis of a dessert for serving after a light meal, yoghurt offers a satisfying and nutritious treat, especially if it is made from raw goat's milk. By choosing pure blackcurrant syrup concentrate as the natural sweetener, a significant quantity of vitamin C is also made available.

NO COOKING REQUIRED SERVES 4

INGREDIENTS

4 suitable parfait glasses
2 cups plain goat's milk yoghurt
40 g natural currants
½ cup pure blackcurrant syrup concentrate
4 pecan nut half kernels

METHOD

1 To each parfait glass add ½ cup yoghurt.
2 Add 10 g currants and a quarter of the total syrup to each glass.
3 Use a parfait spoon to lightly swirl the currants and syrup into the yoghurt.
4 Place a pecan half on top of each glass.
5 Put the completed parfaits in the freezer to chill for 15 minutes.

ALTERNATIVES

1 Pure grape syrup concentrate or cherry concentrate can be used instead of blackcurrant.
2 If currants are not desired, this dessert is delicious without added fruit, or with chopped pieces of macadamia nuts.

TO SERVE

This dessert is nicest served slightly chilled on a warm summer's night. For anyone seeking a very light meal, this parfait can serve that function quite admirably.

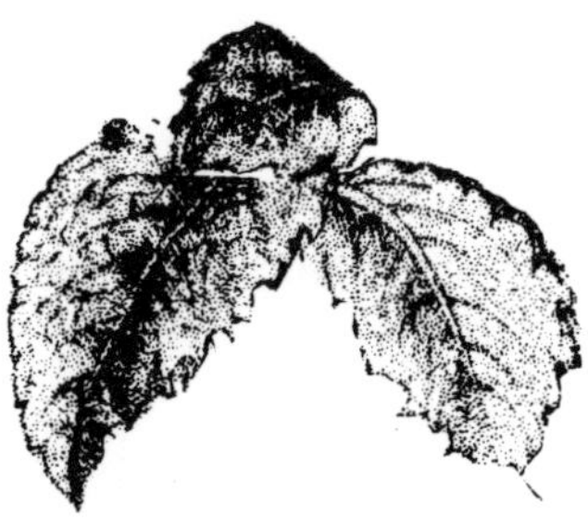

BUCKWHEAT–BANANA PANCAKES

The manifold nutritional virtues of buckwheat have already been described throughout this recipe book, as has the versatility of this important grain. Here is yet another application by which the unique flavour of buckwheat has long been a favourite in America. Buckwheat pancakes do not provide the most nutritious utilisation of the grain, but when one seeks to enjoy a few pancakes for a light meal, there is no more nutritious (or delicious) way of having them. Including banana gives additional pancake flavour; by using soya milk powder, animal milks can be avoided. Topping with maple syrup completes the "American dream", but only pure maple syrup is used here, whereas its very expense usually prohibits its use by commercial eating houses.

GRIDDLE (FLAT HOTPLATE) REQUIRED PREHEATED — MAKES 12 PANCAKES
BLENDING REQUIRED

INGREDIENTS

1½ cups fine buckwheat flour
1 small very ripe banana
3 large open-range eggs
¾ cup pure water
1 tablespoon instant soya milk powder
3 tablespoons cold-pressed vegetable oil
pure maple syrup in jug on table for topping

METHOD

1 Put in a blender all the ingredients except the maple syrup and 1 tablespoon oil.
2 Blend together at three-quarters of full speed until smooth (about one-quarter of a minute).
3 Cover the hot griddle with the reserved oil.
4 Place 1 tablespoon batter onto the griddle centre and cook until small bubbles appear (about 2 minutes), then turn over and repeat. This first pancake is usually discarded, for it is used to "condition" the griddle plate.
5 Use the same method to cook all the pancakes, each of which should be lightly golden on each side. Use 2 tablespoons of batter for each pancake. The consistency of pancakes can be varied by increasing the quantity of flour or reducing the amount of water for thicker pancakes; opposite for thinner. The size of the pancakes can also be varied to suit personal tastes and size of griddle being used.

ALTERNATIVES

1 If a sweet batter is desired, 2 tablespoons pure maple syrup can be added to blender for mixing.
2 If maple butter is obtainable, an additional deliciousness is provided when each hot pancake is thinly spread with it before being stacked for eating. Still pour a little pure maple syrup atop. Maple butter is heat-whipped maple syrup.
3 Other fruit butters (available in many health food stores) can also be used.

TO SERVE

Heap 2 or 3 onto each plate and top with maple syrup for a complete light meal.

CALIFORNIAN DATE PIE

As British as Big Ben and even older is the concept of the pie. Since medieval times, people have found that the convenience of a pastry covered meal has saved them many hours of food preparation. And so it was not surprising to find in the seventeenth century the emergence of the dessert pie. Americans soon grasped the concept and loaded it with apples; and now no self-respecting cook in America cannot bake an indigenous apple pie. From this developed the idea of an open pie, with pastry only on the bottom and sides. Thereby emerged two other famous American pies: the pecan pie and the sweet pumpkin pie. Now here is the beginning of a new fashion in pie baking — indeed it is a first in many ways. This is an unbaked pie; it utilises the wholesome Californian dates; and its pastry is not made from flour. It is as delicious as it is nutritious.

NO COOKING REQUIRED   BLENDING REQUIRED   MAKES 1 MEDIUM PIE

INGREDIENTS FOR CRUST

1 cup raw wheat germ
½ cup desiccated coconut
2 tablespoons cold-pressed vegetable oil
2 tablespoons raw cashew butter

INGREDIENTS FOR FILLING

2 tablespoons instant soya milk powder
2 large apples, washed, quartered and cored
2 medium bananas (ripe), peeled and cut in halves
1 teaspoon ground cinnamon
350 g pitted Californian sun-dried dates
½ cup pure water

METHOD

1 Pour the wheat germ and coconut into a large mixing bowl.
2 In a small mixing bowl, pour the oil and cashew butter and thoroughly mix them.
3 Pour the oil–cashew mixture into the larger bowl and mix thoroughly with the wheat germ and coconut, working them together with the fingers.
4 Brush a little oil around the inside of a 20 cm shallow pie dish.
5 Line the inside of this pie dish with the crust mixture, packing it flat and evenly against the sides and bottom.
6 Put the pie dish in the freezer for 45 minutes to set the crust.
7 When the crust is ready, prepare the filling in the blender.
8 Place in the blender in order: soya milk powder, apples, bananas, cinnamon, dates, then water.
9 Blend at full speed until the mixture is smooth (about 1 minute).
10 Pour the filling into the pie dish and spread evenly.
11 Return the pie to the freezer to set.

ALTERNATIVES

1 Fresh pears can be used instead of apples in the filling.

2 A tasty and compatible decoration for the pie top is pecan nut half kernels. Place them on top before final freezing.
3 If additional spiciness is desired, sprinkle a little ground nutmeg on top before final freezing.

TO SERVE

Keep the pie in the freezer until 10 to 15 minutes before serving. Cut it into serve-sized pieces immediately it is taken from freezer and place on plates ready for serving. It can be served immediately from freezer if desired, but care should be taken when eating to ensure adequate mastication and avoidance of a possible stomach pain from too much frozen food (for this is a very "more-ish" dessert). This pie can be refrozen safely, for it contains only natural ingredients. Nutritious enough to constitute a light meal on its own, this dessert can also be served with fresh fruit salad (but avoid acid fruits), or topped with Blended Banana Cream (page 39).

BLUE PUMPKIN PIE

It is not the pie that is blue, but rather the variety of pumpkin used in this sweet version of the favourite vegetarian recipe. Queensland blue pumpkins are quite versatile vegetables, yet rarely are they considered as being suitable for anything other than main-course serving. Many health-conscious people would otherwise overlook this dessert, owing to the usually sugary nature of the conventional American pumpkin pie. This recipe also avoids the usual use of animal milk (using soya milk) and relies on dried fruits and pure maple syrup for natural sweetening; its crust is also uniquely health-oriented, being free from butter or margarine, even avoiding flour to give a new taste thrill (as is done for Californian Date Pie).

PREHEAT OVEN TO 175° C (345° F)
PRESOAK RAISINS
BLENDING REQUIRED
STEAMING REQUIRED
MAKES 1 LARGE PIE

INGREDIENTS FOR CRUST

1½ cups raw wheat germ
¾ cup desiccated coconut
3 tablespoons cold-pressed vegetable oil
3 tablespoons raw cashew butter

INGREDIENTS FOR FILLING

150 g natural seeded raisins
½ cup pure water
500 g fresh Queensland blue pumpkin
¼ cup cold-pressed vegetable oil
4 tablespoons instant soya milk powder
4 tablespoons pure maple syrup
3 large open-range eggs
1 teaspoon ground cinnamon

METHOD

1 Presoak the raisins in the water for 2 hours.
2 Cut the pumpkin into large pieces, retaining the skin, and steam until tender.
3 Meanwhile, pour the wheat germ and coconut into a large mixing bowl.
4 In a smaller mixing bowl, pour the oil and cashew butter, and thoroughly mix them.
5 Pour the oil–cashew mixture into the larger mixing bowl and mix thoroughly with wheat germ and coconut, working them together with the fingers.
6 Brush a little oil around the inside of a 23 cm shallow pie dish.
7 Line the inside of this pie dish with the crust mixture, packing it flat and evenly against sides and bottom.
8 Peel the pumpkin, cut into chunks, and put in the blender jug.
9 Add the water and raisins, oil, soya milk powder, maple syrup, eggs and cinnamon to the blender and blend at three-quarters of full speed until smooth.
10 Pour the blended liquid into the pie crust, smooth it and place in the oven.
11 Bake until set (when inserted knife can be withdrawn clean); this usually requires 40 to 50 minutes baking time. Setting will continue after it has been taken out of the oven.

ALTERNATIVES

1 If a variation in sweetness is desired, add a very ripe large banana to the blended mixture and reduce the maple syrup to 2 tablespoons.
2 A sprinkling of ground nutmeg on top of the pie provides a tasty variation.
3 Sultanas or dates can be used instead of raisins.
4 Pecan nut half kernels can be used to decorate the top before baking for another tasty variation in flavour and texture.

TO SERVE

This pie should be served cold. Ideal storage, once it has cooled after baking, is in the refrigerator. It can be served as a dessert following a carbohydrate-concentrate meal, but it should not follow a protein-rich meal, as this might lead to indigestion from the high level of fructose in the stomach. This pie can also be served as a complete light meal, topped with Blended Banana Cream (page 39) or similar.

ALMOND CHEESE CAKE

In a significant departure from the usual concept of a cheese cake, this recipe has been conceived to provide the delightful flavour and smooth texture usually associated with cheese cake, together with definite nutritional properties and freedom from digestive inhibitors, consistent with the purpose of this book. Being an uncooked recipe, maximum vitamin values are retained; being a frozen dessert, maximum keeping qualities prevail; being free from refined sugar, flour, butter and margarine, this is truly a health food recipe.

NO COOKING REQUIRED BLENDING REQUIRED MAKES 1 LARGE CHEESE CAKE

INGREDIENTS FOR CRUST

1½ cups raw wheat germ
¾ cup desiccated coconut
3 tablespoons cold-pressed vegetable oil
3 tablespoons raw cashew butter

INGREDIENTS FOR FILLING

3 tablespoons instant soya milk powder
2 large apples, washed, quartered and cored
2 tablespoons fine carob powder
125 g blanched almond meal
⅓ cup pure maple syrup
200 g ricotta cheese, diced
300 g cottage cheese, diced
¼ cup pure water
¼ cup cold-pressed vegetable oil

METHOD

1 Pour the wheat germ and coconut into a large mixing bowl.
2 In a small mixing bowl pour 3 tablespoons oil, cashew butter; thoroughly mix them.
3 Pour the oil–cashew mixture into the larger bowl and mix it thoroughly with wheat germ and coconut, working them together with the fingers.
4 Brush a little oil around the inside of a 23 cm shallow pie dish.
5 Line the sides and bottom of this pie dish firmly and evenly with the crust mixture.
6 Put the pie dish in the freezer for 30 minutes to set the crust.
7 When the crust is ready, prepare the filling in the blender.
8 Put in the blender in order: soya milk powder, apples, carob powder, almond meal, maple syrup, cheeses, water, and oil.
9 Blend at full speed until the mixture is smooth (about 1 minute). If the blender has a small capacity, halve the mixture and blend separately.
10 Pour the blended filling into the pie dish and spread evenly.
11 Return the pie to freezer to set.

ALTERNATIVES

1 Instead of almond meal, cashew meal can be used (or ground from cashew pieces).
2 For some extra spiciness, sprinkle a little nutmeg or cinnamon on top.

TO SERVE

As Californian Date Pie (page 107).

TROPICAL FRUIT CAKE

With so much of its growing area located in tropical or sub-tropical climates, Australia is a very fortunate country. But too little recognition is given by master chefs and bakers to the fruits produced in the tropics. The vitamin and mineral richness of these fruits has already been outlined and the versatility of bananas in cooking already demonstrated. Now pawpaw is shown in another taste-producing role, combined with pineapple, coconut, and dates in this naturally sweetened fruit cake of the tropics. Another unique feature of this cake is the absence of water, for it is replaced by using fresh pawpaw, which contains 88 per cent moisture.

PREHEAT OVEN TO 175° C (345° F) BLENDING REQUIRED MAKES 1½ KG CAKE

INGREDIENTS

250 g dehydrated pineapple pieces
1½ cups wholemeal self-raising flour
½ cup desiccated coconut
350 g fresh ripe pawpaw
2 large very ripe bananas
2 large open-range eggs
½ cup cold-pressed vegetable oil
500 g sun-dried whole dates, pitted

METHOD

1 Chop the pineapple into small pieces.
2 In a large mixing bowl, mix the flour, coconut, and pineapple.
3 Blend the pawpaw flesh, bananas, eggs, oil, and dates at half speed until smooth.
4 Pour the blended liquid into the mixing bowl with the flour mixture and thoroughly mix together.
5 Brush a little oil over the inside surfaces of a 20 cm-square cake tin to cover.
6 Pack the mixture into the tin, ensuring that no air pockets remain.
7 Put in oven until cooked through (about 1½ hours).

ALTERNATIVES

1 If pawpaw is out of season, use ½ cup pure water and ¼ cup pure maple syrup.
2 If you do not want to use self-raising flour, use 1½ cups plain wholemeal wheat flour and increase eggs to 5 and bananas to 3.

TO SERVE

This cake is designed to be rather moist, so it can be served as a dessert after a light fruit meal or a simple vegetable casserole. The best way to store this cake is in the refrigerator in a covered dish.

CELEBRATION FRUIT CAKE

Why is it that when people celebrate a birthday, engagement or retirement, they buy the "lucky" person a fluffy sponge cake, topped with sloppy aerated (often synthetic) cream and icing whose primary ingredient is refined white sugar? Why must everyone be inflicted with such potential poisoning from these empty calories? Tradition is sometimes hard to break, but here is a positive way of doing so. Next time you seek to celebrate a special event with a rich cake, follow this recipe and be led to the sweetest cake, yet with no sugar in its ingredients; the richest flavour, yet with no milk or butter or eggs; the most satisfying texture, for it is full of nourishing dried fruits. Celebrate and be healthy about it!

PREHEAT OVEN TO 135° C (275° F)
BLENDING REQUIRED

MAKES 1 LARGE CAKE (2 KG)

INGREDIENTS

150 g natural currants
200 g natural sultanas
200 g sun-dried diced peaches
1 cup wholemeal flour
1 cup wholemeal self-raising flour
200 g sun-dried pitted dates, diced
200 g dehydrated pineapple pieces
2 cups pure water
¾ cup cold-pressed vegetable oil
2 large very ripe bananas
100 g pecan nut half kernels

METHOD

1 Presoak the currants, sultanas, and peaches in the water at least 2 hours.
2 In a large mixing bowl, mix the flours with the dates and pineapple.
3 Drain the excess water from the presoaked fruit; retain ¾ cup for use.
4 Add the presoaked fruit to the mixture in the mixing bowl.
5 Blend together the water, oil and bananas until smooth (half full speed for a quarter of a minute).
6 Pour the blended liquid into the mixing bowl with the fruit and flour and thoroughly mix in.
7 Brush a little oil over the inside surfaces of a 20 cm-square cake tin.
8 Pack the mixture into the tin, ensuring that no air pockets remain.
9 Decorate the top of the mixture with pecan kernels.
10 Lightly brush a little oil over top of mixture.
11 Bake in the oven until cooked through (about 2 to 3 hours, depending on depth of tin).

ALTERNATIVES

1 Variations in dried fruits can be quite extensive; possible alternatives include figs, sun-dried apricots, nectarines, and apples (all diced).
2 If you prefer not to use self-raising flour, use 5 large open-range eggs instead, but increase the quantity of plain flour to 2 cups.
3 A rich fruit pudding can be baked by eliminating the self-raising flour, retaining plain flour at 1 cup, and adding 3 eggs and another 200 g dates.

ROLLED OAT COOKIES

More than a mere breakfast cereal, rolled oats are quite versatile in baking for main-course meals, breads, desserts, and biscuits. They are used here as the major ingredient in a combination that offers simple sugars (fructose) with complex carbohydrates to provide a balanced, sustained energy release within the body. These cookies are most suitable as snacks for active people who want something to munch on during the day. Children will especially enjoy them, and parents can feel content in the knowledge that they are giving healthful snacks to the little ones.

PREHEAT OVEN TO 190°C (375° F) BLENDING REQUIRED MAKES 25 COOKIES

INGREDIENTS

2 cups rolled oats
1 cup desiccated coconut
150 g whole sun-dried dates
6 tablespoons instant soya milk powder
4 tablespoons pure maple syrup
3 large open-range eggs
¼ cup pure water
¼ cup cold-pressed vegetable oil
2 large very ripe bananas

METHOD

1 Mix the rolled oats and coconut in a large mixing bowl.
2 Remove the seeds and chop the dates into desired size and mix thoroughly with the rolled oats and coconut.
3 Into a blender jug put in order: soya milk powder, maple syrup, eggs, water, oil, and the bananas cut in halves.
4 Blend at three-quarters of full speed until smooth (about half a minute).
5 Pour blended mixture into mixing bowl and thoroughly mix all ingredients.
6 Use a well-oiled cookie tin or baking flat and make 25 cookie mounds, or a larger quantity if preferred smaller.
7 Bake until cooked through (about 20 minutes, if large; 15 if small).

ALTERNATIVES

1 Presoaked sultanas (100 g) can be used instead of dates.
2 If the chewiness of a nut is desired on top of each cookie, use pecan halves, adding before baking.
3 Other rolled grains (such as millet, rye, barley, corn) can be used instead of, or in combination with, rolled oats.

TO STORE

Keep in the refrigerator in summer or at air temperature in winter, but always keep them in an air-tight jar or container to prevent them from drying out.

COCONUT AND CAROB FINGERS

The fibre-rich properties of both coconut and carob have been brought together in this recipe to provide a special sweet treat that is ideal for anyone suffering from fibre deficiency in their diet. Both carob and coconut are nutritionally versatile, providing a suitable balance of alkalising minerals and vitamins, as well as natural sweetness from their fructose content, which contributes to their valuable use to satisfy the "sweet tooth" of modern youngsters (of all ages). The addition of dates, maple syrup, and lecithin makes this snack a most nourishing one for the occasional special treat.

PREHEAT OVEN TO 165° C (330° F) MAKES 15 FINGERS

INGREDIENTS

100 g solid pure carob block
1 large open-range egg
2 tablespoons pure maple syrup
¼ cup cold-pressed vegetable oil
2 tablespoons lecithin powder
1½ cups desiccated coconut
100 g pitted sun-dried dates

METHOD

1 Soften the carob to pouring consistency in the top of a small double boiler, or in an ovenware dish over an open saucepan of boiling water.
2 Blend or beat thoroughly the egg, maple syrup, oil, and lecithin.
3 Into top of boiler or ovenware dish, add coconut, dates and blended mixture to liquid carob, stirring thoroughly.
4 Pour the mixture into a small shallow baking tray.
5 Bake in the oven for 15 minutes, then remove and allow to set by cooling in the tray.
6 When set firm, cut into desirable finger size and gently lift from tray.

ALTERNATIVES

1 Instead of dates, raisins or sultanas can be used; so can chopped dried figs or apricots.
2 Another alternative to dates is pecan nut pieces or macadamia pieces.

PART THREE

GUIDELINES FOR HEALTHFUL MENUS

The Daily Health Diet

An ideal diet should consist of about 75 per cent fresh fruits and vegetables, and 25 per cent of the "concentrated" foods. This 75 per cent is generally alkaline-forming, and the 25 per cent is acid-forming; this gives a balanced intake to supply the body's nutritional needs.

Fresh fruits and vegetables provide the bulk of man's moisture requirements. They supply water in its purest form, in perfect combination with the nutrients our bodies require for perfect functioning and attractive appearance. Fresh fruits and vegetables supply cellulose (bulk or fibre), vitamins, minerals, and energy-giving sugars. In addition, they contain small amounts of protein and polyunsaturated fats. To obtain maximum benefits from these nutrients, fruits and vegetables should always be eaten naturally ripened and raw.

The body's major suppliers of protein, carbohydrates, and fats are the "concentrates". These are more solid foods with much lower moisture content than fresh fruits and vegetables. These are foods which, by virtue of their higher concentrations of major nutrients, should be eaten in smaller quantities.

The major concentrates are nuts and seeds. These are ideally suited to consumption in their dried raw state and comprise the number one group of foods in terms of protein richness. Next come the grains and pulses. These do not lend themselves so suitably to whole, raw consumption. They do respond excellently, however, to sprouting, as described previously. This is the most nutritious manner by which they may be used in our diet. Alternatively they may be ground into flour and baked, or steamed whole — although neither process permits availability of optimum nutrients. However, so long as they are used in recipes which are free from digestive inhibitors, such as are recommended in this book, grains and pulses can be enjoyed as a pleasant alternative food concentrate. For those who may be unsure as to what "pulses" are: it is the convenient botanical expression covering peas, beans, lentils, foods which come out of pods.

While health is intimately related to diet, diet is not the only factor in health. Diet is an important aspect and the one most frequently abused. Nevertheless, the other vital factors of health must be mentioned: fresh air, clean water, rest and relaxation, sunshine, mental balance and harmony, fasting, and exercise and activity.

A daily health menu consists of simple meals that constitute the vast majority of one's weekly food intake. Then, when going out for a meal or when entertaining visitors at home when a compromise meal is consumed, the body will be able to handle it without being inflicted with a build up of toxic residues, such as occurs with people who do not plan their meals in accordance with natural needs. The ideal diet for general healthy consumption is detailed in Stage 10 of *New Dimensions in Health*, but here I will discuss those occasions when guests are visiting or the family desires "something special" by way of a fancy meal.

The healthy fulfilment of this need has been the primary motivation of this recipe book. Even so, all ingredients, preparation methods, recipes, and menus are of proven nutritional benefits. They have all been successfully "tested" on unsuspecting guests and family members, invariably with the examiners' satisfaction coming in the form of "more, please". Thus are satisfied palate and nutritional health by the deft combination of natural ingredients and our fervent desire to ensure that the good health of all is maintained.

It is the secret intention of this book to contribute towards the improved general level of health of our community at large. And that this can be achieved without any compromise in food enjoyment is a proof awaiting every reader. No one needs to consume processed, chemicalised foods, with their false colours and flavours, to obtain the only goodies the world of food enjoyment has to offer. Nature has it all — we only need to be encouraged to know where to look for it, how to prepare it when found, and what to do with it when prepared.

In the main, this book offers recipes that adhere to the food combining principles that the body finds most suitable to facilitating digestion. These are detailed and charted in Stage 9 of *New Dimensions in Health*, which uses digestive guidelines far beyond the usual suggestions in a recipe book, where taste alone has all too often been the determinant.

Menus for Parties and Entertaining

I have already mentioned that a recipe book is not necessary to guide in the selection of the foods that are natural components of a natural diet. But a recipe book is needed to guide the cook who seeks to expand the functions of eating into the realms of entertainment and celebrating.

There is a special feeling of companionship at a gathering of people sharing a meal in friendship. Then why not share good health at the same time? Because we indulge in dinner parties and banquets to celebrate special occasions, there is no reason for us to lose our understanding of what is meant by "real enjoyment". To enjoy the company of friends at a party or celebration at which excessively rich, highly spiced, overcooked, chemically stimulated, poorly combined foods are served, then to pay the penalty by acute indigestion afterwards, is to spoil the entire purpose of the occasion.

Over the years we have found that some of the most pleasant dinner parties and banquets we have given have been when our non-health-conscious friends and acquaintances have been invited. Our health-conscious friends always enjoy the delicious servings at our dinner parties and banquets, but it is the reaction from our steak-and-potato friends that makes such entertaining all the more fun. They invariably admit that before accepting their first invitation to dine with us, they felt uncertain of being served tasty food in sufficient quantity. To see them gasp at the beautiful display on the table before the meal and to hear them compliment us on its flavour during the meal is to continually prove that we have learned a certain magic in catering for parties and entertainment. Yet it is all quite simply done.

I invite all readers to become our friends and to share the enjoyment of catering for parties with delicious food. Learn to share the thrill that always attends the expressions of satisfaction once the meal is over. You, too, will find that your friends will need very little encouragement to accept a second invitation.

It is not because parties and entertainment occupy such a large part of our lives, but rather because such occasions are very important in our socialising. They can become events that are remembered for years, whereas our daily meals are taken for granted. For this reason, we have devoted a significant part of our recipe development to party menus. But please remember that these are only examples — I would not deprive you of the pleasure of developing your own party menus. I have always found this to be part of the fun of having a party.

WORKING BREAKFAST

(Favourite of Politicians and Sales Managers)

Dairy-Free Muesli Cereal (page 38)
Multi-Grain Sweet Bread (page 82)
bowl of raw cashew butter

or

Sweet Fruit Salad (page 4)
Muesli Muffins (page 86)
bowl of raw tahini or cashew butter

POOLSIDE LUNCHEON

(Served Smorgasbord Style)

Savoury Potato Salad (page 24)
Natural Finger Salad (page 15)
Carrot and Raisin Rye Bread (page 80)
Rolled Oat Cookies (page 114)
fresh bananas

or

Tropical Treat (page 3)
Sweet Fruit Salad (page 4)
Low Calorie Fruit and Yoghurt Salad (page 7)
bowls of various sun-dried fruits
some fresh fruits (not citrus) different from those in salads

CHRISTMAS OR EASTER DINNER

Tahini Salad Cream (as a pre-dinner dip) (page 27)
with raw celery and carrot spears
Cashew Nut Loaf (page 47)
Stuffed Mushrooms (page 57)
Anti-Arthritic Avocado Salad, as side salad (page 16)
casserole of lightly steamed zucchinis, cauliflower, and carrots

FORMAL DINNER PARTY

Drinks: freshly prepared carrot and beetroot juice, served with a sprig of fresh mint,
diluted with mineral water if desired
Entree: Vegetable and Nut Cutlets (small) (page 48)
Aubergine Sauce (page 60)
Main Course: Cottage Cheese Bake (page 53)
lightly steamed brussels sprouts and fresh asparagus spears
Side Salad: Mediterranean Tossed Salad (without ricotta cheese) (page 22)
Dessert: Yoghurt Whirl Parfait (page 105)

CELEBRATION BANQUET

(where a variety of compatible dishes is required for a large guest list)

Spicy Fruit Punch (page 33)
Cabbage and Cheese Rolls (page 50)
Cauliflower Croquettes (page 51)
Protein–Carotene Loaf (page 52)
Eggplant Parmesan (page 56)
Capsicum Caprice (page 67)
Seven Seas Casserole (page 49)
Almond Cheese Cake (page 111)
Penguin Ice Cream (page 97)
Celebration Fruit Cake (page 113)

CHILDREN'S BIRTHDAY PARTY

(a light meal of many sweet, smorgasbord-type foods)

Carob and Sultana Ice Cream (set into individual dishes) (page 98)
Baked Fruit Duet (page 104)
Blue Pumpkin Pie (page 109)
Coconut and Carob Fingers (page 115)
a variety of Health Sandwiches
bowls of fresh fruits and sun-dried fruits

Healthful Travelling

Most people find they invariably put on weight when travelling on any lengthy journey. This is caused by their reliance upon "convenience foods" provided at petrol stations, cafés, take-away shops, bus terminals, and on airlines, compounded by lack of physical activity.

During such periods of travel one's energy requirements are invariably reduced. The greatest energy need is for one's mode of conveyance, and it prefers a specific petroleum product. Just as too much fuel causes the engine of your conveyance to splutter and choke, so will too much fuel in your own engine (your stomach) ultimately cause your body to utter its own characteristic form of protest. For this reason, we should always be choosy about our food.

The ideal food for the human body to consume during travelling is fresh raw fruit. No more delicious "convenience food" was ever invented. And how comforting it is to realise that the same Inventor of the ideal convenience food, called fruit, is none other than the One who invented us!

If you cannot arrange to carry sufficient fresh fruit with you (and this is not always possible between countries), arrange to purchase some during the course of your travels, or at your destination. While it is not always possible to purchase fresh fruit along the road, when travelling by car, there is plenty of space in which to carry our own supply. This is not always possible when travelling by plane.

If only they realised it, plane travellers have no problem in obtaining adequate supplies of fresh raw fruit, so long as they remember to ask for it in advance. Every plane carries plenty of fresh fruit in its first-class section, but for those of us who are part of the vast majority of "economy-class" travellers, no difficulty will be experienced so long as we remember to advise the airline 24, preferably 48, hours before departure time. Even if you do forget, or fail to have time to make such arrangements, I can vouch that there is rarely any problem in obtaining fresh raw fruit on the plane if you remind the stewardess about the fruit in the first-class compartment. To save a lengthy explanation, it is probably most expedient to say that your doctor has put you on "a special whole fruit diet" (I will accept the responsibility for that). You will find that all airlines are eager to please their passengers and will invariably provide your special fruit needs. And it is always quite fascinating to notice how many other passengers and many of the cabin crew look longingly at your juicy fresh fruit, envying your favoured treatment. Indeed, it is favoured when compared with the non-nutritive mush invariably served to economy-class airline passengers.

For those making longer journeys, such as aboard ship, there are no problems in obtaining adequate supplies of fresh fruit and vegetable salads, thanks to the modern storage methods available on board. It is advisable, however, to notify the shipping line some days in advance of your departure that you wish the majority of your food to comprise fresh raw fruits and vegetables.

My own experiences in visiting 75 countries and travelling over 250 000 miles with dozens of different airlines and shipping companies has conclusively proven the advantages of eating light when travelling. Irrespective of the standards of hygiene in the country of your visit, when your diet is basically of raw fruits you are independent of the need for drinking water and of the uncertainty that surrounds the sometimes curious methods of food preparation in certain parts of the world. It is comforting to be assured that one will be free of many of the sicknesses that often plague the unwise during international travelling.

With modern transport the world is at our feet, but only while our body remains upright, not prostrated by unsuitable dietary habits.

Raw Foods for the Recovery of Health

Health problems can often be traced to omitting a significant proportion of fresh raw fruits and vegetables from one's diet. The temptation to tamper with nature's own healthful bounty is encouraged by advertisers and sales promotions with all manner of kitchen gadgetry to sell.

If one is suffering from severe ill health, the ideal immediate correction is to undertake a fast. Follow this by a natural foods diet consisting of at least 75 per cent raw fruits and vegetables. It is not always easy to find sufficient time to permit fasting. It is especially then that fresh raw fruits and vegetables must immediately comprise the basis of the diet.

The guidance of a practitioner qualified in nutritional science will determine the means whereby an elimination diet may be undertaken to detoxify the body. This is done naturally and easily, without any semblance of pain, using specific quantities and varieties of fresh raw fruits and some vegetables. Sometimes the whole foods are prescribed, at other times juices are preferred.

In the natural raw food diet, body toxicity is minimised by the high level of nourishment in the food and the absence of foreign chemicals that interfere with the body's healthful functioning. This assists greatly in rejuvenating the body.

Fresh raw fruits and vegetables are rich in energy-giving fruit sugars, vitamins, and mineral cell salts. Indeed, it is the sugars and minerals that provide most of the delicious and characteristic flavours in fresh foods. Other vital nutrients include small percentages of protein and essential fatty acids, together with abundant cellulose. This provides the vital high-fibre component in the diet.

All fresh raw fruits and vegetables also contain abundant vitamins, so necessary to the proper metabolism of the proteins, carbohydrates, and fats. Again the qualified health practitioner will be aware of the various nutritional properties possessed by each variety of fruit and vegetable and will guide the patient to the diet featuring specific emphasis in particular components to enable his body to remedy whatever imbalance exists.

The cooking of fruits, no matter how carefully it is undertaken, effectively destroys most of their natural nutrients. Sugars are dissolved, water-soluble vitamins destroyed, and mineral salts leached by the high penetration of heat into the relatively porous flesh of the fruit. Indeed, fruit is especially unsuited to cooking, as it becomes little more than a pulpy mass of tasteless cellulose.

Many vegetables are made more palatable by light steaming to soften their tissues. This is especially so for potatoes, eggplant, onions, pumpkin, asparagus, broccoli, and brussels sprouts. Salad vegetables are far better eaten raw, such as lettuce, celery, capsicum, tomato, cucumber and alfalfa sprouts.

If it is possible to exercise choice in the selection of fresh fruits and vegetables, always express preference for those grown organically and ripened naturally. They offer improved nutritional and taste properties, as well as longer storage lives. Pay particular attention to the choosing of bananas, for these are all too often gas-"ripened". In fact, the gassing of bananas merely softens their textures and colours them; it does not allow the correct conversion of starch to sugar to occur. This can only take place when mature green bananas are allowed to ripen naturally and slowly. For this reason, it is always best to buy green bananas and allow them to ripen in a warm spot at home.

If it is possible to choose plant-ripened fruit, the greatly improved flavours will be instantly recognised. This is another important reason for choosing fresh fruits and vegetables grown locally. And what better location for the garden than on your own property? As a bonus to the nutritional advantages of such, the joy of watching food grow and of picking it for immediate consumption is of inestimable value to the metaphysical component of the role food plays in human life, especially in the recovery of health.

Raw Foods for Slimming

At the risk of offending those who are not slim, we must regard being overweight as a form of chronic disease. Indeed, as obesity is allowed to proliferate, many other diseases with far more uncomfortable symptoms are more likely to occur.

Of all the human diseases, obesity is the least chronic and the easiest to overcome. It is not so much a matter of will power as a matter of "won't power". It is extremely rare that overweight is caused by gland problems — unless, of course, we consider the salivary glands to be the problems!

The two dietary factors that precondition obesity may be grouped as the amount of food one eats, and the nature of the food one eats. The problem with overweight people is that they eat a greater volume of food than their body requires, and this greater volume is invariably composed of cooked and processed non-nutritive substances.

When the diet includes a significant majority of fresh raw fruits and vegetables, one's chances of developing obesity are almost zero. The extent to which processed and cooked foodstuffs replace the raw is invariably the degree by which the body develops overweight problems. Without exception, every person who has adhered faithfully to the suggested diet of basically raw fruits, vegetables and primary protein concentrates (raw and unsalted nuts and seeds, alternating with cottage or ricotta cheeses) has lost weight and has continued to lose weight until their optimum body weight has been restored. They have then been able to liberalise their diet if they wish. But most find it so easy to prepare, so nourishing, and so enjoyable that this diet requires no effort of will to stay on it.

For people who wish to lose weight, simple and effective guidelines are set out in considerable detail in *New Dimensions in Health*. But food is not the only factor in obesity. Two non-food factors contributing to obesity can be lack of adequate exercise and lack of adequate emotional control. The accumulation of excess body weight invariably implies the intake of a higher number of kilojoules than are being used. This further implies that the source of those kilojoules is nutritionally unbalanced (such as processing causes in foods). Thus, correction lies in the implementation of improved diet and increased activity. We must realise that "labour-saving devices" are not intended to make us indolent.

In cases of emotional upsets, many people turn to food as a "therapy". They readily adopt compulsive eating as an excuse for drowning their sorrows, but all it does is to create more. Such compulsive eating is invariably the uncontrolled expression of a frustrated gluttony for sweet substances (such as biscuits and chocolates); direct such gluttony onto fresh, raw fruits or vegetables and it will soon abate.

All this leads us to the realisation of just how little command many people exert over their own lives — how easily they react and how readily they fabricate excuses. "The greatest victory of all," said Pythagoras, "is empire over oneself."

Some Helpful Conversion Tables

OVEN TEMPERATURES

°C	100	105	110	115	120	125	130	135	140	145	150	155	160	165
°F	212	221	230	239	248	257	266	275	284	293	302	311	320	329

°C	170	175	180	185	190	195	200	205	210	215	220	225	230	235
°F	338	347	356	365	374	383	392	401	410	419	428	437	446	455

LIQUID MEASURES
(practical approximations)

1 cup	= 250 millilitres (mL)
	= 8 fluid ounces (fl oz) USA
	= 8.7 fl oz Imperial (Australian old system)
	= 12 tablespoons
1 tablespoon	= 20 mL
	= ¾ fl oz
	= 4 teaspoons
1 teaspoon	= 5 mL
	= 0.18 fl oz

FLOUR MEASURES
(practical approximations)

1 cup	= 140 grams (g)
	= 5 oz
	= 8 tablespoons
1 tablespoon	= 17 g
	= ½ oz
	= 4 teaspoons
1 teaspoon	= 4 g
	= 1/8 oz

GRAIN MEASURES
(practical approximations)

1 cup	= 190 g
	= 6.7 oz

FOOD ENERGY

1 calorie	= 4.186 kilojoules
10 kilojoules	= 2.4 calories

Index to Major Ingredients in Recipes

If you wish to prepare a particular food, simply use this index to discover tasty and nutritious ways of doing so.

General Index

To discover more about nutrition and preparation methods, use this index to Dr Phillips' guidelines. For the names of recipes please refer to the Contents on page v.

ALSO BY DAVID A. PHILLIPS:

NEW DIMENSIONS IN HEALTH

Natural health care is older than recorded history — among its earliest practitioners was the famous Greek philosopher and scientist Pythagoras. Yet modern demands on our time and energy are constantly highlighting the need for an even better understanding of ourselves and of ways of caring for our health through natural means.

New Dimensions in Health is a comprehensive guide which expands this understanding and traces the path to a healthy lifestyle. In it David A. Phillips describes all aspects of natural health care including our nutritional needs and every step in food preparation from organically grown crops to cooking suggestions. As well as outlining a wholesome diet, he examines the therapeutic use of health foods and herb teas. *New Dimensions in Health* is a complete guide to good health, energy and happiness.

SECRETS OF THE INNER SELF

The study of numerology had its beginnings in the research of the Greek philosopher Pythagoras, who discovered important recurring personality traits amongst individuals who shared similar "ruling numbers". The "ruling numbers" were directly related to the individuals' birthdates and led Pythagoras to the conclusion that certain numerical formulae lay at the bottom of everyone's personality and behaviour. Pythagoras had discovered a pattern of life forces that affect us all. *Secrets of the Inner Self* shows how this knowledge can be used to better our self-awareness and to achieve a more harmonious balance within our lives on both a personal and environmental level.